THE
LIBRARY ASSISTANT'S
MANUAL

THIRD EDITION

F John Chirgwin

and

Phyllis Oldfield

CLIVE BINGLEY  LONDON

Published by
Clive Bingley Limited
7 Ridgmount Street
London WC1E 7AE

First published 1978
Second edition 1982
Third edition 1988

British Library Cataloguing in Publication Data

Chirgwin, F. John
  The library assistant's manual.——3rd ed.
  1. Librarianship–Manuals–For non-
  professional personnel
  I. Title   II. Oldfield, Phyllis
  020

  ISBN 0-85157-420-3

Typeset in 10/12pt Palacio by Library Association Publishing Ltd
Printed and made in Great Britain by Redwood Burn Ltd,
Trowbridge, Wilts.

CONTENTS

PREFACE

This book arose out of a course preparing candidates for the Library and Information Assistant's Certificate of the City and Guilds of London Institute. It was intended to be an introduction to elementary principles of librarianship for non-professional staff in libraries, and it sought to describe simple library routines in a non-technical manner. Now in its third revised edition it has grown to become a simple introduction to libraries and librarianship for many people in this country and abroad forming a much wider audience than those who work in libraries.

It should still be useful for anyone studying for the Library and Information Assistant's Certificate, the BTEC double option module on Library and Information Work, those engaged upon in-service training courses, and people contemplating a career in libraries.

In this third edition, the text has been completely revised and updated, and the chapters on Public Libraries and Enquiries and Reference Material virtually rewritten. There are new sections on electronic mail, data protection, Open College and GCSE, and some older material has been deleted.

Each chapter ends with a revised selection of assignments designed to test the reader's understanding of the topics covered, many taken from past examination papers. The Further Reading at the end of each chapter has been revised and collected in one sequence at the end of the text.

Acknowledgement and thanks are due to the City and Guilds of London Institute for permission to include questions from past examination papers; to the British Library for permission to reproduce Figure 1; to Alan Armsby, Head of Library Services at Newcastle upon Tyne College of Arts and Technology to reproduce Figure 3, and to Mrs Diana Hough for help with typing.

FJC
PO

ABBREVIATIONS

AACR	Anglo-American Cataloguing Rules
ASLIB	Association of Special Libraries and Information Bureaux
ASSIA	*Applied social sciences index and abstracts*
AV	Audio-visual
BHI	*British humanities index*
BLAISE	British Library Automated Information Service
BLCMP	Birmingham Libraries Cooperative Mechanization Project
BLDSC	British Library Document Supply Centre
BNB	*British national bibliography*
BTEC	Business and Technician Education Council
CAB	Citizen's Advice Bureau
CANS	Citizens Advice Notes Service
CD-ROM	Compact Disk – Read Only Memory
CET	Council for Educational Technology
CGLI	City and Guilds of London Institute
CIP	Cataloguing in Publication
CPVE	Certificate of Pre-Vocational Education
CTI	*Current technology index*
DDC	Dewey Decimal Classification
DES	Department of Education and Science
DHSS	Department of Health and Social Security
DPR	Data Protection Registry
GCSE	General Certificate of Secondary Education
HABIT	Handicapped and Aged Benefiting from Information Technology
HMSO	Her Majesty's Stationery Office
IFLA	International Federation of Library Associations
ISBN	International Standard Book Number
JTS	Job Training Scheme
LA	Library Association
LASIP	Library Association Subject Index to Periodicals

MARC	Machine-Readable Catalogue
MSC	Manpower Services Commission
OED	*Oxford English dictionary*
PLR	Public Lending Right
RLB	Regional Library Bureau
SCONUL	Standing Conference of National and University Libraries
SLA	School Library Association
TTNS	The Times Network Systems
TVEI	Technical and Vocational Educational Initiative
UDC	Universal Decimal Classification
VDU	Visual display unit
WBIP	*Whitaker's books in print* (formerly *British books in print*)

Chapter 1

LIBRARY USERS AND THEIR NEEDS: PUBLIC AND NATIONAL LIBRARIES

The public library movement was launched in this country with the Public Libraries (England) Act of 1850. This act allowed for the establishment of town libraries, which were free and open to all ratepayers and provided by funds from local rates. Because the right to establish such a library on the part of any municipal authority was permissive and not compulsory, many years were to elapse before the entire needs of all the potential reading public across the country were to be served.

A further act, the Public Libraries Act of 1919, gave the opportunity for greatly increased library provision, empowering county councils to adopt the Libraries Act for those districts within their respective areas which had not already done so. The new county library systems established buildings for branch libraries within their respective areas, in the small towns and large villages where no libraries had previously existed. Even in small villages and hamlets, centres were set up in school rooms or other suitable existing buildings, where periodical exchanges of book stock housed at headquarters could be arranged. These libraries were, and still are, organized from a county headquarters, normally sited in the county town.

It was in 1964 that public library provision became compulsory. The passing of the Public Libraries and Museum Act 1964 meant that for the first time all parts of England and Wales were given as of right a comprehensive and nationally linked library service. With local government reorganization in 1974 came changes in the boundaries of public library authorities. Some county branch libraries were transferred to adjacent municipal authorities, and became branch libraries served by the central library of the municipal authority, instead of as formerly, by the county headquarters. But whether under the auspices of a county or

1

municipal authority, and of whatever size or type, all public libraries continue as the Kenyon Report (1927) proposed that they should, 'to serve not only the earnest seekers after knowledge, but also all those who are. . .gratifying an elementary curiosity, and those who are seeking relaxation and recreation.'

To have the library of his choice both easily accessible and open when he is able to use it, are obviously the first requirements of any potential borrower. It is essential that public libraries are sited centrally in their respective cities, towns or villages, preferably on or near main roads which give access to public transport, and where car parking facilities can be made available. Many central libraries are now built adjacent to or as an integral part of a shopping complex. In this way such libraries are assisted in both attracting and retaining their borrowing public.

Similarly branch libraries are sited centrally in their respective smaller towns and villages, offering a representative though necessarily more limited selection of library services to their borrowers. Such libraries act as access points to the full range of resources that are housed in the central libraries with which they are linked. In the same way, mobile libraries serve the needs of readers living in the more remote areas, giving such people entry as of right into all regional and national resources.

It has become the practice for libraries to make lecture and meeting rooms available to serve the needs of the local community, and to support an immense variety of extension activities. Rooms are booked for such purposes as the running of WEA (Workers Educational Association) classes, the giving of public lectures on subjects of current interest and concern, whilst the National Trust for example, and local groups such as ornithologists, local historians and others can hold slide and film presentation evenings. Foyers and entrance halls are used for the mounting of exhibitions such as arts and crafts, and photography on the part of local organizations and institutions. The local Citizen's Advice Bureau (CAB) is often housed in or adjacent to the public library. In many directions therefore, the library, in the various purposes it serves, becomes the focal point and cultural centre of its own neighbourhood.

The lending department
Once he is inside the building, almost certainly the first person

to make contact with the potential borrower will be the library assistant, who is given an excellent opportunity for performing a very useful public relations exercise. A good first impression of the library often stems from the tactful ways in which the discerning assistant can provide information, help with form filling and so on. Sensitivity to the individual needs and indeed fears of differing personalities is needed. Older people in particular are often lacking in confidence, and can be helped by unobtrusive guidance. The written formalities completed, some people appreciate being taken on a quick tour of the library, by the library assistant who is able to point out where their special interest areas are to be found. For those who prefer to explore the library for themselves, a wall plan of the library floor, or floors, should be provided. In addition, a printed floor plan can be incorporated into a handout or guide which is made available to all new library members. Such a guide will include, in addition to the floor plan, information about the library, its rules, services offered, borrowing facilities and so on.

A library guide serves the needs of its borrowers by explaining how books can be borrowed, and for how long. It indicates the procedures for reserving books, and tells how requests for new additions to the library should be made. It informs readers of the inter-library loan network, demonstrating the fact that all libraries, however small, are part of a nationally linked scheme. It explains how the particular library classifies and catalogues its stock and lists all the non-book materials that are available. It also draws attention to any specialist services offered, such as photocopying. It enables borrowers to locate books not in normal sequence on the shelves for reasons of size or specialist subject matter. Finally, it states clearly all the essential rules relating to the lending of books and to general use of the library itself.

It is necessary to draw readers' attention to the catalogue. Many people are unaware that they can consult it since they imagine it is solely for the use of library staff. A library catalogue, whether consisting of five by three inch cards in drawers, or of computer microfiche, needs to be augmented by displayed instructions concerning its handling. The latest type of catalogue now being brought into use is that in the microfiche form. Provided that sufficient reading machines are made available for its usage, many more readers can consult a microfiche catalogue at any one time than can those consulting a five by three card catalogue. Moreover the microfiche form facilitates easy and constant updating of the catalogue on the part of the cataloguing staff. It is becoming increasingly common for school classes to visit their public library, where they are taught, amongst other skills, how to handle the catalogue for themselves, and also how subjects are inter-related. Since the microfiche format is being brought into use in many areas of industry, commerce and information services, developing children's skills in this way serves a dual purpose. This area of work could well be extended: many older people and others, such as the unemployed with more leisure time available, would welcome talks on how to use their library and its resources to the full. There would also be the opportunity to practise the handling of the various microforms and the utilization of the appropriate reading machines.

The larger public libraries aim to provide a readers' advisory service point, where the borrowers' specific information needs can be met. Here all the bibliographical aids are to hand, to enable the adviser to answer questions concerning titles of books in print, and of newly published books not held in the library. The *British national bibliography (BNB)*, *Whitaker's books in print (WBIP)* and *The bookseller* are always available to serve these purposes. Many libraries pride themselves on supplying book lists of special categories of books, drawn up by themselves. Lists of the historical and science fiction books available, for example, are much appreciated and used by borrowers. Often a library will compile its own book list on a topical theme, thus highlighting books that otherwise might remain unnoticed and unknown in their normal sequence on the shelves.

Another way in which libraries can highlight particular categories of books and thus demonstrate a theme that is common to all of them, is by mounting displays. A 'House maintenance' exhibition gives an opportunity to bring together books dealing with such varied subjects as decor, electricity, joinery and soft furnishing which are normally separated by the classification scheme on the shelves. Such a display demonstrates inter-relationships between subjects more directly, and with greater impact, than can the library catalogue. Displays can also link a library and its books with the outside world and its variety of other media. Readers are given the opportunity to broaden and deepen interest, through having their attention drawn to books that have formed the basis of radio or television broadcasts. Again, displays planned to coincide with local events draw attention to other community activities, giving opportunities to demonstrate the connections linking the many and varied local recreational, cultural and educational activities.

Many libraries amass a considerable amount of community literature, some of which is kept on permanent display. Examples of such literature are careers information, educational courses handouts, and information handouts on where to go for advice and assistance of all kinds. Smaller libraries sometimes provide a diary which can be used by local organizations to publicize their own events and activities and which is particularly useful for new members of the community to consult. Further demands are now being made on public library resources and study accommodation by the number of open and distance learning programmes now being developed. One of the earliest of these was the Open University, which aims to extend and widen educational opportunities for mature adults. Public library opening hours are now having to be made more flexible to meet the demands of such working students.

Increasingly, attention is being paid to the needs of particular client groups which public libraries serve, in order to ensure the provision of appropriate, relevant services. This has resulted in many constructive developments in what is now referred to as community librarianship. Such libraries now offer advice on benefits, employment, careers, housing, pensions, consumer affairs and other similar matters, or put people in touch with other sources. The needs of ethnic groups, the unwaged, hospital patients, prisoners and other groups are being constructively considered and thus met. Many public libraries now serve ethnic community needs by support and advice from joint voluntary committees. Multi-media collections are being provided, including in addition to books in other languages, cassettes, records and videos, resulting in the library's provision being enriched for all users. Multi-cultural book fairs are featuring relevant material for such collections, whilst publishers are increasingly providing dual language books for children and adults.

Services for handicapped persons are being increasingly developed. The needs of readers housebound by physical

5

disability, or made immobile by increasing age, are met by a supply of reading material from a van delivery service. Now a further community resource has been developed to assist in serving handicapped and elderly people. The Reading HABIT (Handicapped and Aged Benefiting from Information Technology) provides a quick request service. Using a monitor or terminal, participants can send a message via Prestel to their respective library headquarters. The requested books are then dispatched to their nearest library, or even for home delivery where necessary.

To its great credit, the public library sector has responded well to the nationally mounted Adult Literacy Campaign, with its implications for a different type of book provision. The official adult literacy sign is displayed in many library lending departments, drawing attention to a range of easy reading books of all types. Individual members of staff are being encouraged to specialize in this sensitive and highly important area of work.

Finally, the lending departments of the larger public libraries are increasingly offering items other than books for loan; the most common being pictures, records, cassettes, computer software and video recordings. It is usual to allow pictures to be kept by one borrower for a period of roughly three months and to make a small charge for each picture that is loaned. Some libraries issue records and cassette tapes free of charge whilst others ask for a small fee per item borrowed, or else offer an annual subscription rate which covers the cost of borrowing any number of items within one year. Another service is that offered to those wishing to teach themselves a language. Kits made up of cassette tapes, instruction books and worksheets, can be loaned for use at home or in the library. Some libraries offer video lending services for which they make a charge. Charges are also made in some instances for computer database searches, heavy overdue fines are levied even on children's books, and many libraries look to these charges to offset declining budgets. It is becoming increasingly difficult to offer a service that is based on the principle of full access to information and education for rich and poor alike.

The reference department

A public library also serves the needs of those seeking information, and therefore provides a reference department or, in the case of a smaller library, a reference section. Books and other material provided here must of necessity be on hand for consultation at any time; therefore they are not as a rule available for loan. This department will house books of a general nature that deal with many subjects, such as encyclopaedias and collections of newspaper cuttings. It will also house books that for a variety of reasons cannot be allowed out on loan. Rare books, certain large size books, e.g. atlases and collections of photographs, expensive books, out of print and irreplaceable works can all come into the category of 'reference books'; as can standard works on specialist subjects which people may wish to consult rather than read from cover to cover. In the interests of economy, large reference departments are increasingly drawing on a variety of computerized systems for the retrieval of information requested by users. Two such systems are referred to in more detail in Chapter 2.

The reference department is also the one which holds local history collections, consisting not only of books, but in addition old maps, documents, cuttings collections, guide books, booklets and pamphlets. Archives, i.e. local records and other manuscript documents relating to local institutions, form a part of such a collection. Current local information is also kept on file, and lists of addresses of local government departments, religious and social bodies and societies are made available.

Publications issued by government departments, statistical information, and Acts of Parliament can all be consulted. Hansard, which is the official report of debates that have taken place in parliament, is available at least in the larger reference departments. In addition, the reference department, unless the library is large enough to warrant the provision of a separate commercial and technical department, will also contain all the appropriate quick reference material in which will be included telephone, street and trade directories, bus, train and air timetables, yearbooks, gazetteers, guide books and bibliographical aids of all kinds. Effective use of all these reference sources can only be made after training and much practice. Library assistants should aim to develop an awareness of the source materials available, a knowledge of what they contain and the ability to locate quickly the particular items of information that are required. (See Chapter 9 for examples of reference materials.)

Commercial and technical departments

The central public library located in a large town or city generally provides an additional department usually known as the commercial and/or technical department. This serves the needs of commerce and industry in the area as well as the needs of individual citizens, and those of visitors from outside the area. Information seekers in this department are likely to request very specific items of information, and many enquiries are made and dealt with over the telephone. Teletext television services such as Ceefax and Oracle, and viewdata services such as Prestel, provide such departments with up-to-the-minute local, national and international news and information.

The commercial department carries company information of all kinds concerning locally based firms and also national ones and their subsidiaries. The quick reference materials such as trade directories, timetables and yearbooks are to hand in this department of a large library. Collections of materials relating to other countries, notably in the areas of industry, commerce and travel, are also available. Specialist information of concern to companies is supplied including works on company law, patent specifications of recent inventions and British Standard specifications relating to manufactured products. Large-scale maps and street plans of the locality and surrounding areas may be consulted, as may current traders' lists and catalogues.

This is generally the department where current and back copies of daily, Sunday and local newspapers are kept, along with a range of magazines, journals and periodicals both of a specialist and a general nature. Newspaper provision aims to cover a balanced political spectrum, whilst magazines and journals are reviewed from time to time to ensure the broadest possible range of professional and recreational reading. Recently, there have been attempts to disagree with library selection policies, and by implication with the impartial judgement of librarians, particularly on the question of newspaper provision. The banning of *The Times* newspapers by some local authorities has been a case in question. This has been challenged by the Library Association on behalf of its members, and it is now becoming accepted that such imposed censorship is alien to the whole principle of library service and provision. Back copies of newspapers and periodicals are held for a specified period usually ranging from one to five years according to the lasting value of their contents. The most important periodicals of all are bound into yearly volumes which become part of the permanent book stock. To enable the borrower to trace articles relating to specific topics from periodicals and magazines, appropriate indexes, e.g. *Current technology index*, are to hand. Once such an article has been traced, it is usually possible for the borrower to obtain a photocopy of the article, since a photocopier is now usually considered an essential feature of such a department. Some departments provide also the machines which give copies of material that is in microfiche and microfilm form.

The children's department
The children's department has first to satisfy the recreational and leisure needs of its readers by offering a wide ranging and well balanced fiction, non-fiction and reference book stock. It often augments the educational resources which are available to the child in school and elsewhere, through the provision of both book and non-book materials, and is organized in such a way as to ensure that its readers automatically transfer to the adult section of the library when the time arrives.

Even the youngest children are made welcome in the library. Such children, accompanying parents on their visits, are given picture books to handle and to take home on loan. Books are placed in low standing browser boxes in strategic corners of the main lending department or else in the children's department itself. The provision of low chairs or floor cushions encourages children to become involved with the books. Story telling and story reading sessions are arranged for pre-school children, and these draw attention to the connection between the spoken and the written word.

Although school is the place where the majority of children learn the mechanics of reading, not all schools are in a position to provide the wide range of imaginative, stimulating story books needed to encourage the child to put his newly learnt reading skills to the fullest use. Likewise many secondary schools, whilst providing non-fiction books appropriate to the school curriculum, do not always provide the spread of fiction that would be appropriate in order to cater fully for the needs of their particular pupils. There is a special onus therefore on the public library to provide the fullest possible coverage of good children's literature. Librarians, anxious to make the transfer from the children's to the adult department as smooth as possible, often create a 'young adults' fiction section within the children's department. This enables young people to sample novels from a specially selected range of adult fiction, without being overwhelmed by the size of the main collection.

Children's and young people's services librarians, through their skilled selection of books and other resources, aim not only to ensure that their stocks develop and continue to be maintained to the highest standards, but also that children are made aware of what is available to them. Children's Book Weeks are promoted both nationally and locally, when exhibitions, competitions, and a variety of activities are arranged. Children's authors and illustrators are invited to come along, and to share their own world with their young audiences. Such promotions do much to encourage children who have never done so before, to join their local public library; as also do holiday events that are organized during school holiday times by the children's libraries staff. Many libraries now promote the services they offer through the sale of a variety of items such as T-shirts, bookmarks, pens, booklists and the like, to which are added appropriate captions, thus producing an extra source of revenue. A variety of extension activities, such as book clubs, competitions and quizzes also help to publicize the stock and the work of the department.

A children's reference section has always traditionally been headed by a selection of the best children's encyclopaedias. Nowadays information exists in increasing quantity and comes from a variety of sources through an ever increasing range of media. It is widely recognized that pupils must learn how to learn, and that a central feature of this process is knowing how to deal with information. For this reason, many more demands are now being made on the public library, its resources and its staff. Children at both primary and secondary level are being asked to carry out projects and assignments which involve them in both searching out and processing relevant information. Some libraries build up their own kits to help children in their search for information. These comprise not only newspaper cuttings but also photographs, maps, charts, photocopies of letters and documents, all relating to one theme.

With the introduction of General Certificate of Secondary Education (GCSE) courses which will be followed by most secondary school pupils, even greater demands will be made on all types of library resources. Of particular importance will be collections of up-to-date information on a wide range of topics. These will necessitate the provision of cuttings files for ephemeral material, microfiche, online links to external computer databases such as Prestel and The Times Network System, statistical data, video recordings, interactive video sources such as the BBC Domesday Project, audio tapes, slides and computer software. The information management skills of librarians will be much in demand, as the course becomes established, in the planning and provision of appropriate resource facilities and services, and in the professional assistance given to both teaching staff and pupils.

These then are the main ways in which the public library aims to satisfy the explicit needs of its wide ranging readership. A forward looking library, however, must not fail to be constantly exploring new developments in areas for which the library has not hitherto made provision.

National libraries
National libraries are generally copyright or legal deposit libraries; that is by law they are entitled to receive a free copy of all material published in their respective countries. They undertake the classification of the material and the preparation of national bibliographies. They also serve in the capacity of national agents in the field of international library cooperation. The office of the International Federation of Library Associations and Institutions (IFLA) administers an international lending system based at Boston Spa.

The British Library is said to be one of the world's three largest national lending libraries, the others being those of the United States and the USSR. In this country the British Library was formed by Act of Parliament in 1973, and three main divisions set up to cover its lending, reference and bibliographic services. A more recent restructuring has resulted in the following regrouping of services (see Figure 1).

The Bibliographic Services Division's role is to record a wide selection of the printed material in English acquired by the Library. It lists all significant publications in the *British national*

11

Figure 1

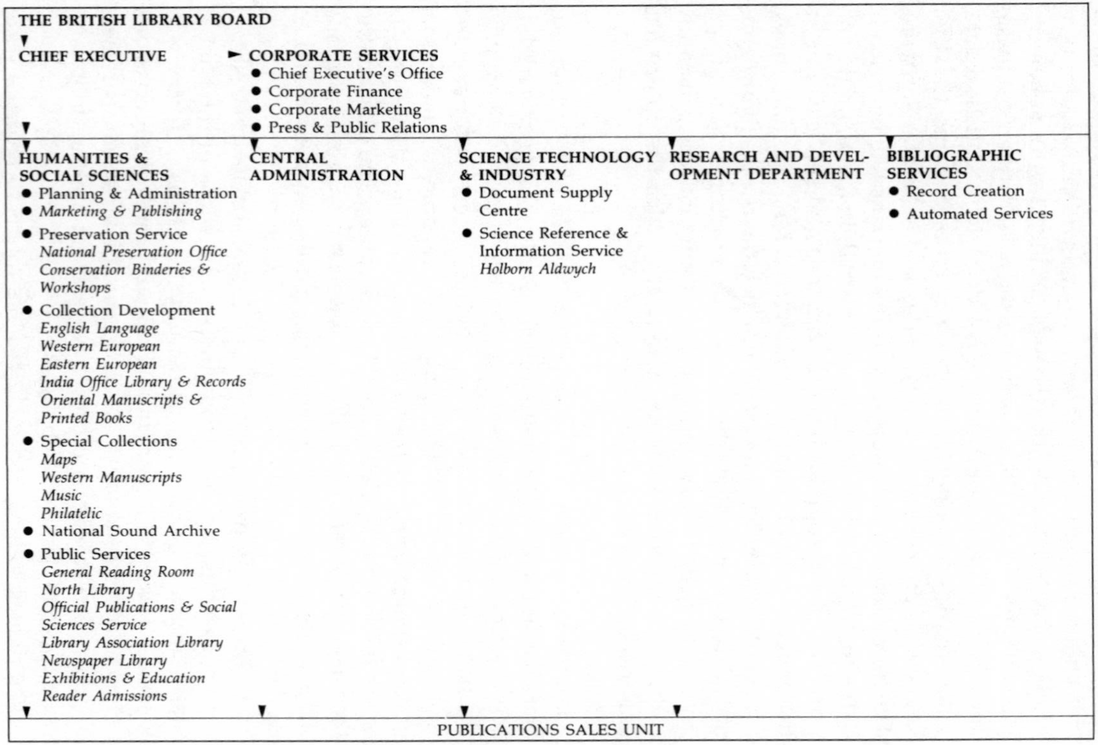

THE BRITISH LIBRARY BOARD

CHIEF EXECUTIVE → **CORPORATE SERVICES**
- Chief Executive's Office
- Corporate Finance
- Corporate Marketing
- Press & Public Relations

CENTRAL ADMINISTRATION

HUMANITIES & SOCIAL SCIENCES
- Planning & Administration
- Marketing & Publishing
- Preservation Service
  National Preservation Office
  Conservation Binderies & Workshops
- Collection Development
  English Language
  Western European
  Eastern European
  India Office Library & Records
  Oriental Manuscripts & Printed Books
- Special Collections
  Maps
  Western Manuscripts
  Music
  Philatelic
- National Sound Archive
- Public Services
  General Reading Room
  North Library
  Official Publications & Social Sciences Service
  Library Association Library
  Newspaper Library
  Exhibitions & Education
  Reader Admissions

SCIENCE TECHNOLOGY & INDUSTRY
- Document Supply Centre
- Science Reference & Information Service
  Holborn Aldwych

RESEARCH AND DEVELOPMENT DEPARTMENT

BIBLIOGRAPHIC SERVICES
- Record Creation
- Automated Services

PUBLICATIONS SALES UNIT

12

bibliography. It also publishes the *British catalogue of music,* the *British education index* and *Books in English.*

The Research and Development Department encourages and supports library and information research and its dissemination by funding projects and publishing their results.

The Document Supply Centre at Boston Spa is concerned specifically with interlending and its work is more fully described in Chapter 8: Lending procedures.

The Science Reference and Information Service covers the former Science Reference Library housing the major UK reference collection of scientific and technological literature, including the former Patent Office Library.

The Humanities and Social Services Division was formerly the Reference Division comprising the Department of Printed Books, the Department of Manuscripts and the Department of Oriental Manuscripts and Printed Books.

The National Sound Archive aims to preserve and record all kinds of recorded sound including music and wildlife sounds. Important publications include their *Discographies of British composers.*

The British Library also houses the India Office Library, the Library Association Library, collections of maps, music, newspapers and ephemera such as posters, postcards and greetings cards.

In order to meet the requirements of a national library system for the twenty-first century, a new building is planned for central London which will rehouse most of the British Library's present functions under one roof. This building will eventually replace all the Library's present land and buildings, but not the Document Supply Centre, formerly the Lending Division, which operates from Boston Spa in Yorkshire.

Assignments
1   Write a short essay on the type of users, their reading needs and how these can be met, in a public library.
2   Take any *two* of the following departments of a large public library, and compare/contrast the ways in which borrowers' needs are met in each of them:
    a the lending department
    b the reference department

c the commercial/technical department

d the children's department.

3 Suggest the steps that a public library could and should take to ensure that pre-school children and school children become adult users of the public library in their later lives.

4 How do national libraries differ from other types of library? Answer with particular reference to the ways they are funded, the services they provide and the people who use them. (CGLI 1986)

Chapter 2

LIBRARY USERS AND THEIR NEEDS: EDUCATIONAL AND SPECIAL LIBRARIES

University libraries

Some university libraries have been built up over the centuries; others have come into existence over the last 40 years. It is hardly surprising therefore that big variations are to be found in both the size and the contents of university libraries. The older universities, naturally enough, tend to have the largest collections, but all university libraries aim to cover the range of disciplines read at their respective establishments. The post-war period saw a great increase in the numbers of university undergraduate and postgraduate students, the consequence of which was the establishment of seven new universities. It became increasingly necessary for the country's university libraries to become more closely coordinated. In 1950 the Standing Conference of National and University Libraries (SCONUL) was founded 'to represent the interests of member libraries by providing a forum for the exchange of information and collaborative effort'. By 1967 the University Committee on libraries was being briefed to report on 'effective and economic arrangements' for book and periodical provision in universities and other higher educational institutions. This report, which became known as the Parry Report, proposed the establishment of a British national library. Another result of the report was the setting up of the framework for inter-library cooperation amongst university libraries themselves, and between them and public libraries.

Users

Previously the provision of book and other materials for purposes of research had been considered of paramount importance. With the dramatic increase in the number of post-war students, it came to be more generally accepted that a university library should aim

15

to serve the needs of three main categories of reader, namely the undergraduate, the research worker and the academic staff. For the undergraduate the provision of multiple copies of text books is usually considered essential, as is the provision of as many copies as can be afforded of recommended background reading. It is more difficult to provide for the needs of research workers, since not even the researcher himself can predict what items will be required. Libraries build up collections of manuscripts, archive material, monographs (i.e. treatises that deal with single limited subjects) and theses that have been submitted by previous students. They also keep a range of abstracts and indexes that give sources of information concerning research articles. Not only does such provision form the basis for a particular student's research; it also shows him what research has already been undertaken in his particular field, and thus enables him to avoid duplicating work already covered.

Increasingly university libraries are making reciprocal arrangements with their city libraries and with those of other educational institutions. One library will undertake to buy certain expensive items and make them available on loan for readers from other libraries. Long sets of periodicals not in constant use can be covered by such an arrangement. Similar arrangements are in hand for the coverage of foreign literature: thus duplication is being avoided and money saved.

Countrywide there are many examples of local and regional cooperation among other universities and higher education institutions generally. In several regions such schemes are arranged to work alongside the BLDSC distribution system.

Readers' services

It is essential that all users of the university library know firstly, what their particular library contains and how they can obtain it and, secondly, what outside agencies have to offer and how that too can be obtained. To this end, printed guides explaining the layout and the contents of the library and the services provided for readers are given to all new members. In this guide, attention is drawn to the library's catalogues, and in addition to union catalogues which indicate the stock carried by other libraries which can be drawn upon by readers. Many libraries issue a separate guide which explains the classification scheme that is used, and sets out in detail how the catalogue can best be consulted. Other libraries have large notices displayed which demonstrate (by means of diagrams) how the catalogue can be used. When searching for material, the normal procedure for many students is to scan the appropriate shelf and it is therefore important to demonstrate by all possible means just how the catalogue can be such an essential reference tool. It alone can show them the complex relationships that exist between subjects; it can also carry as many cross-references as are thought necessary to draw the attention of every potential reader to whichever book they require.

In addition, the library collections of large universities are often housed on several different floors or even in different buildings. The central catalogue, by giving location references for all its entries, helps readers to find out where particular books are housed. It also indicates any books which are out of sequence for any reason, as when, for example, a library has built up a special collection of books relating to one subject. This is known as an 'in depth' collection which is often, on account of its size, housed in a separate area away from its normal sequence on the shelves.

Bibliographical materials are also part of readers' services. These enable readers to trace not only details of books, but also of periodical and newspaper articles. They include not only general bibliographical sources but also the bibliographies that deal with the literature of particular subjects as well as the specialist periodical abstracting services such as *Chemical abstracts* and *Psychological abstracts*. Increasing numbers of university libraries are presenting both catalogues and bibliographical information in computer microfilm, microfiche, or cassette tape form, and explanations as to the handling of these new forms have to be given.

Specialist library tutors are employed who explain the use of the library and give assistance in the tracing of literature sources of a particular subject. Classes and seminars are also given in the use of abstracts, bibliographies and works of reference in a specialized field. Such tutors work closely with academic teaching staff, and in some cases with members of staff who have been chosen to liaise between the library and particular departments. Such liaison not only extends the possibilities for readers' services work, but can also assist in improving standards for book selection.

Special facilities
University readers, who are usually living away from home, need study facilities to be available to them for long periods of the day and evening. Most of their libraries offer 9.00 a.m. to 10.00 p.m. opening on weekdays, and a somewhat curtailed opening day on Saturdays. Library services are also offered in vacation time. Libraries usually arrange separate areas where current periodicals, maps, government publications, early printed books and manuscripts are housed. Each such area has its own arrangement, so that students are able to work adjacent to their own source material. Because much of the stock of a university library is available for reference only, it is important that facilities for photocopying material, and for obtaining copies of information in microform format, are made available for the direct use of students.

If books are allowed out on loan it is of crucial importance that a student should not keep books longer than necessary to complete an essay, for instance. Such books have to be zealously guarded by library staff in the interests of other students who may well be required to write an essay on the same subject at the same time. Libraries make special arrangements for short-term loans lasting as little as two hours in some cases, and charge heavy fines to act as a deterrent to defaulters. Lastly, some university libraries are now providing what are known in the United States as 'browser collections'. Such collections set out to cater for the leisure needs of students as well as for their professional needs, by providing material for recreational reading.

College libraries
The single term 'college library' covers a broad spectrum of further and higher education, ranging from those housed in colleges of further education, to those in polytechnics and colleges of higher education. Detailed definition of the purposes and functions of such a variety of libraries is beyond the scope of this present book. Colleges of all types do, however, have one common aspect: their respective libraries have developed in response to the demands placed upon them by the needs of their students, both of a

professional and an individual nature. The majority have been established over recent years as a direct response to their needs.

By comparison with universities, where the majority of students are undergraduates pursuing full-time courses, many colleges house a constantly changing population of full-time, part-time, day release, sandwich course and evening class students. Such colleges are generally closely associated with local industry, commerce and the professions, and they are increasingly concerned with 'selling' their courses in the market place to such employers. The library, as an integral part of a college's central services, therefore becomes an important selling point for the courses on offer. These cover a wide area, ranging from craft courses for all types of industry, GCSE and 'A' level subjects, General, National and Higher National Certificates and Diplomas, to degree, professional and post-graduate work. The Manpower Services Commission (MSC) promotes a number of college courses for the unemployed and/or school leavers, such as the current Job Training Scheme (JTS).

As a result of the focus of attention on open and distance learning, 'Open College' broadcast programmes are now being prepared, and courses offered for mature adults at technical and supervisory levels of skill and knowledge, and others which promote personal development and leisure interests. In this way, the needs of those such as shift workers and the housebound who are prevented from attending normal college courses for a variety of reasons, are now being met. Students follow individual learning programmes at their own pace, using open learning materials and drawing on library resources in a variety of ways. College staff offer counselling and tutorial services on an individual basis, by telephone or correspondence where necessary.

Whatever the subject area, range or level of the respective courses, the college library must aim to cover them. Background knowledge and information on course-taught subjects will be available, as well as general and quick reference material, including bibliographical aids to both book and periodical searching. Since much material is now presented in microfiche, audio-visual and computerized formats, students receive instruction from tutor-librarians on their use, and are also shown the range of information sources relating to their particular interest or subject area. Most college libraries also aim to cover subjects such as General Studies and Communications, general background reading and current affairs, and to offer a selection of English and foreign literature. The setting up of the Business and Technician Education Council (BTEC) resulted in a range of college courses being offered at General, National and Higher National levels. Project assignments and an information-based, problem-solving approach play a major part in all three levels of courses, making increased demands on college library resources.

Audio-visual resources are now provided on such a scale that many colleges both house and administer such resources in a separate audio-visual or resource centre. Other colleges retain a direct link between the library and the resource centre by housing them in adjacent areas.

College and polytechnic libraries often serve their local communities by making their resources available to local business organizations and industrial firms. Technical literature and information is provided on request. Colleges of Higher Education aim to cover the needs of their students by the provision of book and non-book materials relating to education, the school curriculum, teaching and learning methodology, professional practice and standard works dealing with the various subject areas covered. Resource materials serve not only the students' course needs, but also act as a reserve bank which can be drawn upon when students are engaged on fieldwork or work experience.

School libraries

Unlike public libraries, school libraries are not run according to any nationally directed policy. Consequently there are wide variations in the ways in which they are financed, organized and serviced. Even so, school library provision has been improved and increased out of all recognition since the days when only the long established grammar schools and public schools had libraries of their own. The public library service has always included provision for children and young people in its aims, and this provision has included not only work done in the children's departments of public libraries, but also that done in the schools lying within the administrative area of the public library.

With the passing of the 1964 Public Libraries and Museums Act, when the whole of the country's public library service came under the supervision of the Department of Education and Science, an opportunity was given for a more closely integrated service to be developed between library authorities and education authorities. In practice, however, the greatly increased numbers of school libraries and the quality of those libraries owes much to the enthusiasm and hard work of teachers in schools, to librarians who specialize in work with children and young people as well as to the cooperation, both official and unofficial that goes on between these two groups and their respective organizations.

The Library Association had until 1937 a subsection known as the School Libraries Group. Although in 1937, this subsection was withdrawn from the Library Association and became known as the independent 'School Library Association' (SLA), the Library Association continued to have links with the SLA whilst also promoting work with children and young people within a subsection of its own, now known as the Youth Libraries Group (YLG). The School Library Association's aims are: 'to promote the use of the school library as an instrument of education and to encourage efficient methods of administration and exploitation.' It recognizes the relevance and importance of both books and non-book resources, and seeks to provide opportunities, through local and national activities, for cooperation and exchange of experience among school librarians and others. Only recently, however, the Library Association has revived its own subsection for its members who are engaged in school library work, and now once again has its own School Libraries Group (SLG).

Schools library services

A survey undertaken by the Library Association in 1967 showed that the majority of school library services are administered by the public library service on an agency basis for the education authorities, and are financed through the Education Committee. The survey also found that most county libraries work closely with schools, as do many, though by no means all, the municipal library authorities. In the case of the county libraries, the schools library service is usually based on the county library headquarters, whilst in the case of the municipal library authority it is based on the central public library.

The schools library service is generally planned in consultation with the appropriate education department. It offers collections of books and materials on permanent, long-term or short-term loan to schools of all kinds. It provides a projects service whereby collections of material on a given topic (including, in addition to books, such items as topic kits, wallcharts, filmstrips, illustrations) are delivered to schools to supplement the school's own resources. A travelling van not only delivers the books to be lent; it also acts as a place where book selection can be undertaken by teachers and in some cases by the children themselves.

This service, usually in the hands of a qualified and senior librarian with supporting staff, provides a variety of formal and informal professional advisory services to schools. These include the organization of exhibitions and activities for children, for parents and for teachers. It also offers general bibliographical facilities and a wide range of printed aids, including specialist book lists. In addition it provides help with book ordering, and in many cases undertakes the processing of books, so that less time is taken up in schools with such tasks.

It is now becoming common for public library authorities to provide separate resource libraries from which schools may borrow a wide range of non-book materials as and when required. Similarly many authority owned museums have lending departments which arrange for replicas and non-valuable items to be available for schools.

Primary school libraries
In the past decade or so, much stalwart work has been done in order to provide non-textbook reading material for primary school children. Some primary schools have opted to gather their library book stock into one central place, and to administer the contents in roughly the same way as does a public library. Others have chosen to surround children with books in whatever area of the school they happen to be, believing that books should be on hand at all times so that a child's search for knowledge is not hampered in any way.

Many infant and junior schools have books in the entrance hall and in the corridors as well as in the classrooms. In the classrooms reading corners are arranged where books are attractively displayed on easily accessible stands, and where children can sit comfortably and enjoy their reading activities. Some primary schools classify non-fiction books by using the simplified schools edition of the Dewey decimal classification scheme. Others feel that even the simplified Dewey is too complex for young children to use, and have chosen to use colour coding to indicate a book's subject, all science books having a blue label òn their spine, all history red ones, and so on.

Because primary school numbers are generally smaller than those of secondary schools, book funds are also correspondingly smaller, since schools are given an allowance per head of school population. As a primary school pupil gets a much smaller book allowance per head than a sixth former, say, a primary school book fund goes no way towards providing a fully stocked library service. Extra money for books is raised in a variety of ways, not least through the efforts of active parent/teachers' associations. Also, since primary schools do not employ full-time librarians, the library collection usually being run by a teacher with responsibility for library work, the schools library service for its part pays particular attention to the needs of primary school libraries, visiting and supporting them more frequently. Public libraries including branch libraries, in the vicinity of primary schools, offer valuable supporting services in the way of loans for projects, exhibitions, displays and talks on library usage.

Secondary school libraries
Great impetus was given to secondary school library work with the passing of the far-reaching Education Act of 1944, which proposed secondary education for all children as of right. The new schools, provided in order to implement the act, listed library facilities among their essential requirements, and the work of building up library stocks to meet the needs of the new type of school curriculum began. Beginning with some London schools, several authorities started to employ professional librarians in schools, whose job it was to set up and maintain the school library, and to exploit its resources to the best advantage in collaboration with the school's teaching staff. Other authorities chose to make a teacher responsible for the school library, giving him or her an extra responsibility allowance for so doing. At the present time there are a number of courses which enable a professional librarian to become qualified as a teacher and vice versa, and it seems possible that in the long-term future all school librarians could be dually qualified in teaching and librarianship.

The library and the curriculum

Secondary school libraries not only reflect what is taught in schools but also how it is taught. At the present time broad themes or areas of work are taught in an integrated way, each subject teacher working in a team, having his own contribution to make to the overall theme. The library or what is now often referred to as the school library/resource centre, provides both book and non-book materials for such teaching. By so doing it can demonstrate to pupils the interrelationship that exists between subjects, whilst at the same time the materials provided act as a stimulus to the pupil's imagination. Moreover, much emphasis is now put on the child learning rather than the teacher teaching. Project work and 'discovery' learning methods demand that library provision is made for children in both primary and secondary schools working independently either as individuals or in small groups.

Of recent years, curriculum changes resulting in the new GCSE and amended 'A' level courses have required many pupils to prepare projects and other independent assignments. The setting up of sixth-form colleges has also seen the introduction of courses based on technical and vocational training, of which the Certificate of Pre-Vocational Education (CPVE) and the Technical and Vocational Education Initiative (TVEI) are recent examples. Again, such courses emphasize the need for the widest possible provision of independent learning facilities and resources. Over the past decade, increasing attention has been focused on educating students in the use of library and other resources. The British Library has funded several research projects in this field. It is now becoming accepted that library skills could and should be taught in conjunction with associated study skills, and that both teaching and library staff of educational establishments should be working together to formulate a joint school/college policy that incorporates the practice of such skills into the whole school curriculum.

Outside school links

There are many opportunities for the secondary school library to demonstrate its links with the outside world. It can provide university and college prospectuses, printed material on all aspects of careers and their selection, and examination requirements of professional bodies. It should accumulate all the free material distributed by the industrial, commercial and banking organizations in the area and make sure that these are kept up-to-date. The library also carries sources of information about outside visits likely to be undertaken by schools and offers background reading material concerning the places to be visited. It also holds information about the local community which can be of both a permanent and an ephemeral nature. Active parent/teachers' associations can be valuable providers of such information, and some volunteer parents are prepared to assist in the classification of the material provided. Pupils' work undertaken as a project or a report can similarly be usefully incorporated into the library's permanent collection. In all these various ways the school library serves the needs of its users; and by so doing endeavours to ensure that its readers continue to use their public libraries in the future.

Special libraries
This is a term generally accepted as covering a variety of types of library other than public and educational. Libraries associated with commerce and industry, with research associations, government departments, learned societies, professional associations and with corporate bodies, can all be said to come under the heading of 'special libraries'. The overriding require-ment of the special library is that it should provide current information that enables research workers and other employees to carry out their company duties effectively. Therefore it provides not only a collection of material for which there is a known demand, but also a network of services that make information readily available from a variety of outside sources. ASLIB, founded in 1926 as the Association of Special Libraries and Information Bureaux, and which is independent of the Library Association, has done much to promote and support this kind of library work. ASLIB's aims are 'to facilitate the coordination of any systematic use of sources of knowledge and information in all public affairs'. Included in the bureau's 2,000 membership in addition to the special types of libraries listed above are some national, academic and public libraries. It was during the Second World War that urgent attention was focused on company research work. This in turn led to a big expansion in the library

services which of necessity had to be provided for the research and information requirements of company personnel. ASLIB was recognized as being an essential body requiring government support.

Company libraries have much more clearly defined terms of reference than have the previous types of library we have been considering. For a thriving industry, investment in a library information service is essential if it is to remain competitive with its rivals in this country and abroad. Such a service can be the joint charge of librarians and scientific information officers who are specialists in the literature and other sources of information of a particular subject.

Reference services
Selection of the relevant up-to-date reference materials is essential in order to provide the service their users require. Unlike public libraries, where book selection is in the hands of the librarian, here book and other resource selection is often the domain of the research worker himself. In collections of this kind, bibliographies, periodicals, abstracts and indexes are more prominent than books. Much of the reference material is in the form of unpublished reports, trade literature, press cuttings and handouts. The contents of the reference sections of special libraries vary according to the needs of the particular organization. Science and technology orientated libraries for example provide the British Standards specifications and Codes of Practice that relate to the products of their respective companies. Information about patents is made available, and a service provided whereby patents can be scanned so that a close check can be kept on new developments. Commercial libraries, on the other hand are likely to provide company documents and annual reports, along with market surveys and economic reports. Any large special library will provide, in addition to its specialist materials, such items as laws and regulations, conference proceedings and a variety of statistical information and government publications.

Journals and periodicals
Company personnel need to be kept abreast of developments in their own and in related fields: they also require information about work being done in other companies. Therefore a range of

scientific, technical and trade publications issued weekly, monthly, quarterly or irregularly is provided. An abstracting and indexing service offered by the staff ensures that the user is informed of what relevant papers and articles are available to him, whether in their original form, recorded on microfilm or microfiche, or forming part of a bound volume. Some libraries display their journals but indicate that they are for reference only, whilst others, anxious that articles should not be missed by potential readers, allow the periodicals out on loan by means of a circulation list. In order to provide information not covered by their own stock, most sizeable special libraries join the subscribers' service offered by the British Library Document Supply Centre (BLDSC) housed at Boston Spa in Yorkshire. This division now heads a national interlending system currently carrying a stock of some two and a half million books and periodicals which can be borrowed or photocopied and over one and a half million documents on microform. Over 70% of the requests made to BLDSC relate to science and technology. Photocopies of articles and papers can be obtained virtually by return of post, and the BLDSC service also provides translations of foreign articles when required. Associated with BLDSC are 14 back-up libraries whose large resources supplement BLDSC's own collection. In addition to this national network it is possible for libraries to draw on their own regional interlending system. Moreover special libraries have tended to form their own local cooperative schemes with other organizations working in similar fields, finding that this can result in a speedy service to the user.

Information searching services

Library and information staff carry out searches daily, some of which are undertaken as a matter of routine, or when specific information is requested by users. Routine searching operates for example when national and local newspapers are scanned, and cuttings files prepared about a particular company or a particular product. Staff also keep users informed of what is available by compiling bulletins that give annotated lists of recent publications, together with other news of interest to them. This is known as an alerting service. One internationally known and widely used alerting service is that produced on behalf of the US Institute for Scientific Information, which is known as *Current contents*. The weekly issues of this publication alert readers to the titles of papers and articles about to be published in the relevant specialist journals, which cover between them the full range of sciences; medical, physical and chemical, social and behavioural, and engineering.

Many libraries are now engaged in mechanized computerized searching which can save much time. The computer, linked to databases, is programmed to produce a list of all co-related articles or books published on a particular subject. This is achieved by feeding the computer with one or more keywords representing the subject under research. 'The Lockheed Information Systems of the USA', known as DIALOG, is one example of a system widely subscribed to by libraries in this country which are extensively engaged in searches. DIALOG's 'bank' consists of 100 major bases that cover scientific, humanities and business subjects. The costs involved in consulting such databases can be considerable. Since 1977, one of the two major functions of the British Library Automated Information Service (BLAISE) has been the provision of an automated information retrieval service. This was conceived as a means of cutting down the cost of online searching, and this has been achieved by giving subscribing libraries access to BLAISE through the national telephone system. The databases already cover medicine and related sciences, environmental pollution, chemical substances, education, and the preparation of further databases is under way.

Systems which use a television receiver to communicate information to viewers (videotext) are being widely adopted for use in industry and in the business world. One such system, for which a specially adapted TV receiver is required, is a teletext service whose operation is one way, i.e. the viewer may only await the display of pages continually broadcast in cyclic sequence from the database. These systems provide as a free service a wide variety of regularly updated information under such headings as news, finance, business news, weather, travel, sport etc. The BBC's teletext service is known as Ceefax, whilst that of ITV is known as Oracle. A further system, operated by British Telecom and incorporating the use of a TV receiver, keypad and the user's telephone dial, is known as Prestel. In contrast to the teletext system which is one way, Prestel is a viewdata two-way (interactive) system, utilizing the TV screen to present information specifically requested by the user. The Prestel computer database stores millions of pages of information, and these are being added to and updated continually. A subscriber to the service uses a code index in order to locate the information required; the code is dialled by telephone or input by keypad and the appropriate page of information is projected on to a TV receiver. The user can also use his keypad to reply to the system (in a limited fashion). The subscriber is charged for the telephone call, for certain items of information requested, and for computer time in gaining access to a page. When this system becomes fully operational, almost limitless information could be made available to subscribers.

Assignments
1 What are the particular skills required of information officers or librarians in special libraries? How does their role differ from that of librarians in public or academic libraries? (CGLI 1986)
2 What is Prestel? Assess its significance as an aid to answering reference enquiries. (CGLI 1986)
3 Outline the range of supportive services which could be drawn upon by the librarian of a comprehensive school library.

Chapter 3

ORGANIZATION AND ADMINISTRATION

Most libraries are responsible to higher authorities. Overall responsibility usually lies with the governing body of an institution or a local authority. It is this higher authority which ultimately controls financial and staffing matters, without which no library can function adequately.

In local authorities, public libraries are established in accordance with acts of parliament. The Public Libraries and Museums Act of 1964 lays down the legal framework under which public libraries operate in England and Wales. Briefly, the act places responsibility for public libraries on the Department of Education and Science, and sets up two Library Advisory Councils to assist the minister responsible. Local authorities have a statutory duty 'to provide a comprehensive and efficient library service for all' and the service must be freely available.

Local authorities appoint committees to administer their responsibilities in certain ways. Library matters are usually delegated to a special library committee, although they may well share a committee with some other allied sphere of interest. The chairman of such a committee will be its leader, and library spokesman in council. He acts as an intermediary between the librarian and the other elected members, and his knowledge of fellow councillors, overall policy and work on other committees, and interests will be extremely valuable. The chairman controls discussion in committee and should be well versed in all library matters. The committee will decide matters of policy and planning, and the librarian is responsible for carrying out the administrative functions which make policy a reality. The librarian will report to his committee on a regular basis such matters as staffing, finance and extension activities. This is his opportunity to promote the needs and potential of the service. The librarian cannot decide policy, but he can initiate ideas and suggest possible courses of action for the committee to consider.

The modern trend is towards much larger areas of committee responsibility. Some local authorities have adopted systems of corporate planning which involve the setting up of several management divisions. Libraries are often included in divisions with leisure, recreation and other public amenities. An overall director is appointed to each division with assistant directors responsible for each area of interest. This results in many chief librarians holding second or even third tier appointments, and thus losing direct access to their committees. On the other hand, many librarians have been appointed to directorships with increased responsibilities over a wide range of activities. Senior library staff are also expected to play a significant role in the planning, development and reviewing of library and other services, so that a properly corporate approach to problems can be followed at all levels of the service.

In educational libraries, similar management techniques are often encountered. There is usually a library committee to decide policy and to advise on library matters such as finance and staffing. In smaller libraries, such as schools, and in industrial libraries, government and control may be vested in one person, e.g. the headmaster, or research director, and this can lead to more effective control, depending on the persons involved. The problems encountered, however, are unlikely to be as complex or as formal as in local authority services.

Finance

Money plays a crucial role in the administration and development of libraries. The extent and the quality of the library service will depend largely on the finance available since it is this which determines the provision of buildings, staffing and book purchasing, and a great deal of time and effort goes into ensuring that the money available is properly used and recorded.

Public libraries are financed mainly from local and central government sources, the main sources of income being local authority rates, central government loans and grants, and charges for services and accommodation. However, there are plans to replace the present system of rates with another form of local taxation or community charge which will be levied across a wider cross section of the local population. Each year, the librarian must present an estimate of his financial requirements for the next year. These annual estimates may be in two parts. The first relates to items of capital expenditure, which usually include major projects such as new buildings or building extensions, and the purchase of very expensive items such as motor vehicles or computer equipment. The second part concerns the revenue expenditure which consists mainly of recurring items such as staff salaries, book fund, gas and electricity, transport, repairs and maintenance, loan charges, and consumable items. The revenue estimates therefore include all the day-to-day running expenses of the library, and the capital estimates include the major, permanent, non-recurring costs.

The estimates are prepared by the librarian, with the help of finance officers from the treasurer's department, and are submitted to the local authority's library committee for approval. They are then considered by the Finance Committee, and possibly by the Personnel Committee if there are staffing implications, before being approved at a meeting of the full council. When the estimates have been examined and approved in this way, they become the official limits of expenditure for the service for that year. It is then the duty of the librarian to ensure that expenditure is kept within the limits of the appropriate headings, and to administer the amounts allocated as wisely and effectively as possible. The administration of the budget may be subject to inspection by local authority and central government auditors.

In educational libraries, similar estimates of expenditure are calculated and go forward for approval by the various committees concerned. University libraries estimate their requirements against the background of expenditure for the university as a whole. Other educational libraries prepare estimates, with the overall budget of the college or school very clearly in mind. Industrial and special libraries also work on an annual basis within the framework of the needs and requirements of their institutions.

Staffing
An efficient and busy library will depend considerably on the calibre of staff that are employed. Public libraries often have to cope with an increasing volume of work, in the form of larger numbers of new books and issues. Therefore, the work needs to

be highly organized and consistent, involving many routine processes. Long opening hours with mealtime and evening service and staff interchanges emphasize the need for efficient, well trained staff, who are sympathetic to readers.

It is one of the chief librarian's duties to determine how the library shall be run, and to ensure that it is being run properly and efficiently. The first step is to review the whole of the library's operations to see what services are required, and how they can be provided. Then the number of staff needed to meet the requirements can be assessed. The librarian prepares a list of the numbers and kinds of posts needed, with their appropriate grades, duties and responsibilities. These are approved by the appropriate governing body and become the staff establishment of the library concerned. A structure or framework of posts is thus created with varying emphasis according to the relative size and importance of each area of work.

There will be one chief librarian, who is mainly concerned with the direction and leadership of the service as a whole, and who will spend much of his time on committee work, reports, correspondence, and other administrative duties. In large library systems there may be more than one deputy or assistant chief librarian to supervise the general running of the library and to deputize for the chief when necessary. Various senior assistant librarians will take charge of major sections of library services such as reference, children's, cataloguing and lending departments. There will be senior librarians in charge of services based on geographical areas in large public libraries, and each full-time branch library will have a qualified librarian in charge. In addition there will be several assistant librarians to support their senior colleagues, trainee librarians who are not yet fully qualified and up to 60% of established posts may be filled by library assistants, who perform most of the front line tasks in contact with readers and with the physical provision of materials for the library shelves. A modern development has been the introduction of many community projects sponsored by the Government through the Manpower Services Commission. These have included several employment initiatives aimed at specific problems or at providing opportunities for particular sectors of the workforce, such as school leavers or the long-term unemployed. These MSC initiatives have proved to be an important addition to the staffing

33

resources available to libraries and other organizations also, and many valuable and useful projects have been undertaken as a result.

From time to time, vacancies arise or new posts are created and need to be filled. Most vacant posts are advertised to allow all interested persons to apply, usually in writing. When all the applications have been received a short list of candidates is chosen, and these may be invited to attend for interview for final selection. Each new appointee should be given a job description which outlines their duties and responsibilities and indicates how this post fits the staffing structure and overall working plan. Salaries and conditions of service are negotiated and agreed nationally in public libraries, with perhaps some local variations for evening and Saturday duties. Most large libraries have properly conducted training programmes for new appointees including talks and practical demonstrations by senior staff, attendance on short courses or day release facilities at their local further education college, together with visits, staff interchanges, meetings and conferences. Large libraries will try to keep staff informed of administrative and professional developments by regular staff meetings, newsletters and bulletins. Some libraries have properly constituted staff associations which meet for educational and social activities. In smaller libraries, daily routine tasks may not be so time consuming and repetitive and this also offers a greater variety of work and experience. Most library duties still remain to be done, but the volume of such work decreases, making fewer specialist posts necessary.

Organization
Most library activities fall into three or four categories which can easily be identified and which help to form a functional framework. Library administration involves most financial, staffing and building matters, in addition to planning and development programmes. It also includes the review and analysis of all procedures, and the clerical and administrative duties common to most libraries. Bibliographical work will consist of acquisitions, book processing, classification, cataloguing and perhaps binding. Reader services will include the normal lending and reference work and may also cover library publications and inter-library cooperation. Extension activities, exhibitions and

publicity work may be prominent enough to form another section.

Public libraries
Most public library systems now serve wider areas and larger populations than before, and with the introduction of larger library systems and corporate management techniques, administrative services have become increasingly complex and are often housed in central corporation offices away from the main libraries. Frequently, bibliographical services are housed in a library headquarters, which again may be central and separate, since little direct work with readers is undertaken here. Most municipal libraries will have a large central library, usually in the centre of town, with large bookstocks and several departments. There is always a lending library for adult readers, and usually a children's library also. There is a reference library and this will probably be the most important reference collection in the district and the centre for all reference and information services, handling enquiries from the public, from branch libraries and from other sections of the service.

A large specialist local history library is usually part of the reference service, and sometimes commercial and/or technical libraries also exist. Some large city libraries adopt a subject departmental approach, and there may be specialist library collections for music, social sciences and the arts in addition to the most commonly encountered subject arrangements. Branch libraries serve their immediate locality. Full-time branches offer lending services for adults and children, with possibly a quick reference collection of the most frequently used material. Part time branches and mobile libraries offer a lending service on a more modest scale. Various services to special categories of readers may include visits to the housebound, hospitals, prisons and schools.

County libraries often have the problems of serving large areas, with relatively small populations, since the more densely populated areas are served by municipal libraries. The major disadvantage of large areas is that bookstocks become more thinly spread and depth of coverage becomes difficult. Several methods can be used to improve the situation and these methods reflect themselves in some county library practices, which are not usually needed in the towns. Often, many more copies of titles are purchased, and the allocation and recording of bookstocks may be more complex, especially if books are circulated from branch to branch, or exchange and mobile collections are frequently revised. There will be a greater reliance on communications, transport and postal services than in the towns, and because there may be no central library, reference services in particular may suffer from the lack of a large centrally held bookstock. Reference and information services are usually carried on from county library headquarters, in addition to book requests and interlibrary loans. Some counties and large municipal libraries have adopted a regional framework, where branches and staff are grouped together, and bookstocks merged for wider and more specialized coverage. In some areas, certain administrative functions have been delegated to regions, to give local staff and residents more participation in the running and organization of library services.

Education and special
Most educational and industrial institutions prefer centrally situated library services. However, the larger universities and polytechnics may be located on more than one site, and if so library facilities will also be dispersed, although administrative and technical services will be centralized. Many site libraries offer reader services in a particular faculty or subject area. Large industrial firms may also have libraries associated with the work of their various divisions. In the smaller libraries, work is varied since all aspects of library services are encountered. Staffs of two or three undertake most library duties, and share a more varied role, specializing in closely defined subject areas.

Assignments
1 Describe briefly how public libraries obtain their finances.
2 Outline the methods used in a large library to communicate information on matters affecting the library service to all members of staff.
3 Describe the differences between the stocks and services of a reference department and those of a lending department of a large public library. (CGLI 1970)
4 List *five* departments one would expect to find in a large municipal central library. Describe briefly the functions of one of these. (CGLI 1972)

5 Draw an organizational chart showing the management structure of the library/information unit in which you work. Indicate your position on the chart, and briefly explain the flow of work between professional and non-professional staff. (CGLI 1986)

Chapter 4

ACQUISITIONS AND STOCK RECORDS

Most library books are obtained either by purchase, exchange or gift. They are purchased mainly from booksellers and not directly from publishers, except in the case of certain specialized reference works. There are three main types of booksellers: first, the specialists who may cater for foreign books, or children's, or special subject material. Next there are the general bookshops known to the general public. Then there are also the library suppliers who offer large collections specially for public and institutional libraries, and who do not sell to the public. Periodicals may be bought from local newsagents, or from library supply agencies specializing in foreign and academic journals. Some periodicals may be obtained from societies and firms individually.

Book ordering
Most library books are bought on approval, which means that they may be returned if they are unsuitable. After the initial selection has been made, order cards are usually made with full details included. Missing details are found and others verified by checking in general bibliographies such as *Whitaker's books in print*, *British national bibliography* and publishers' catalogues. Details such as author, title, publisher, ISBN and price are very important, since they identify the book accurately and mistakes can lead to duplicate ordering. Uniformity of entries is also important in this respect, especially when checking for previous copies. When the order cards are complete they are first checked against the library catalogue to see whether they are in stock, and then in the order file to see whether other copies are either on order or in progress. The items to be ordered are allocated to booksellers, and orders are typed on official order forms, which

are then signed and posted to booksellers. Some booksellers send out lists or cards to help with book selection and these can be marked for ordering and returned to the suppliers. Orders can also be placed by telephone, telex or by personal visits, but some authorities require such orders to be confirmed on official stationery. Order cards are now supplied with the name of the bookseller, date of order and order number and are filed in the order files, and the library budget records are amended to include the latest order. The whole operation should be done with consistency and speed. The longer it takes, the more omissions in checking will be likely, as orders flow through the system continuously, and also the temptation to short circuit the procedure for urgent items becomes greater.

In many large educational and public libraries, online computer ordering systems are replacing the older, manual methods. Every book title has a unique International Standard Book Number (ISBN) and this is usually all that is required by the computer to locate the full details by searching the Machine Readable Catalogue Database (MARC). All the necessary checking is done automatically before the computer places the order with a bookseller similarly equipped with online facilities.

Budget records
Records of financial transactions should be kept as simple as possible. The records are to ensure that funds are spent correctly and that the budget is not overspent. It is also helpful in planning expenditure systematically, so as to ensure an even flow of acquisitions.

Each order and each invoice should be recorded separately so that it can easily be seen how much has been allocated for orders, and how much remains, and more importantly, how much expense has actually been incurred on invoices. Many items which are ordered will never be received for various reasons and the invoices passed are the only true record of what has been spent. Unfortunately, invoices usually lag too far behind orders to be reliable records themselves. Orders and invoices should be frequently compared, remembering that one represents estimated expenditure and the other actual.

Financial records should be kept in a way which ensures accuracy. Many libraries keep running totals of expenditure and remainders, which confirm totals when added. Many devise other systems which cross-check similarly and thus eliminate errors. Large authorities keep their accounts by computer or by other mechanical means. Quite sophisticated financial information systems can sometimes be devised, if required, by analysing the accounts according to various factors, e.g. amounts spent per branch library in a large system, or by bookseller, subject, or departments, or physical form – periodicals, audio-visual, books. This is one of the benefits of mechanized accounting procedures.

Exchanges and gifts

Often material may be acquired or offered by exchange through the British Library Gift and Exchange Section at BLDSC. Benefiting libraries are expected to offer similar free publications in return. Gifts of books and journals can often be quite fortuitous. Several bodies produce free material which can be supplied on request. Often this can be a valuable source of information not easily obtained in other ways. Material available from banks and building societies, voluntary organizations, company reports, careers and tourist literature, DHSS and local authority information are all important sources for the local community, and although much of it may be ephemeral it may have a topical importance that needs regular revision. Free material is only worth the trouble if it is appropriate to the needs of the library. Otherwise it becomes just as expensive as purchased items, in terms of clerical work, cataloguing, classification and shelf space.

Receipt

When books are received they are unpacked and checked against the delivery or advice note to ensure that the parcel contains what it is supposed to contain. The books are then checked against the invoice, which describes the goods despatched and states the amount charged. This entails making sure that the prices and quantities are as stated. Some libraries collate books at this stage, but many do not check the physical make up of books at all, choosing to let imperfections show themselves in due course.

The goods received are then checked against the order to ensure that what has been delivered was in fact ordered in the correct quantities and formats. The order cards are located and the date received and invoice number recorded. If a separate progress file is kept, the cards are moved on there, from the order file. Invoices are passed for payment and budget records updated.

Processing
The books are then allocated to branches, classified, catalogued and prepared for the shelves. Most books are plastic jacketed. Date labels are attached and any necessary charging stationery, depending on the type of charging system in use. Spines are numbered with the classification number, and any other local processing is done. For a nominal fee, many booksellers will supply books ready prepared with jackets and the appropriate stationery to suit the requirements of most libraries. Books are then checked with their catalogue entries, preferably by staff from another section, and then displayed or shelved. Some items may be noted for inclusion in book lists or recent additions lists.

Periodicals
The acquisition of periodicals is similar to the procedure for books, but being received at regular intervals, they require special recording. Details are verified in guides and bibliographies, and checked against current holdings and orders. Suppliers are chosen, orders sent and budget records altered accordingly.

On receipt of the first issue of a new journal, the item is checked against the invoice and its corresponding order. The invoice is then passed for payment, in advance of the receipt of the remainder of the year's supply. A record is kept of the order number, date, supplier and invoice details. Each succeeding issue is noted by recording the number of the issue, and the date received in columns corresponding to the date of issue. Many libraries house their periodical receipt records in horizontal index trays, and use coloured markers against a calendar scale to indicate at a glance whether copies are being received on time.

Omissions must be checked regularly and followed up promptly. Usually a telephone call will act as a preliminary reminder, but a letter or pro forma enquiry will probably be useful. A great deal of time can be spent chasing up late copies, or obtaining credit for non-arrivals.

Statistics
All organizations need standards to measure performance,

achievement and efficiency. Statistics provide information to assist management decision making, particularly when changes of systems are being considered. There are many problems in assessing and controlling a cultural or educational service. When using comparisons it is difficult to compare like with like. A good measure of performance is to compare current figures with last year's figures. This should show as accurate a picture as possible, if all variables are taken into account, e.g. population shifts.

The following statistics are usually kept in libraries:
– Number of books purchased
– Number of titles purchased
– Number of books discarded
– Number of books in stock
– Population served
– Number of issues, per service point
– Number of inter-library loans, reservations
– Number of BL applications
– Numbers of types of material, periodicals, records, photocopies
– Daily issues, reference enquiries.

Figures on size of bookstock can be compared with national output, average prices and subject breakdowns and the unit cost of operations or transactions can be calculated, sometimes providing illuminating insights into the cost of various aspects of the service, which could pinpoint problem areas for improvement or investigation. Many of these figures fail to take quality into account, and they must be seen in the light of the library's policy and programme of objectives. Accuracy in recording figures is essential, and any system with cross-checks will ensure accuracy. Running totals are also extremely helpful when information is needed urgently.

Stocktaking

Stocktaking is the physical checking of each book in stock. It is quite a simple exercise where the library is on closed access and some libraries that stocktake close until the operation is complete. Methods of stocktaking vary according to the kind of stock records in use. If an accessions register or a shelf-list exists, then each is useful, especially if recorded on cards. Cards are checked against the shelves, the issue, the stock, binding, repairs and other collections of material in progress. The cards are marked to indicate the presence of a book at stocktaking. Cards for missing books are separated, rechecked at a later date, and withdrawn or replaced. This is probably the simplest way, but large systems can be more complex and the speed of the operation is essential. If the procedures extend over a period of days, the system that is being checked is changing as it is checked, and the results become more and more unreliable.

Many libraries no longer stocktake each year. Some undertake the operation at longer intervals, or as a random exercise. A continuous stocktake can sometimes be tried, by working slowly through stock records when other work permits, although the results may be unsatisfactory. Some librarians doubt the value of stocktaking, since it is a negative exercise which produces nothing. Gaps in stock can be found and covered through requests and reserves, and careful stock revision can eliminate most deficiencies. Stock figures are revised and the catalogue is kept up-to-date. Missing books are indicated, but the losses cannot be stopped, or the books recovered. It is extremely costly in terms of staff time and completely disrupts the library's work while it lasts.

Stock records
The accession register is a record of books added to a library. Books are numbered progressively as they are added to stock and entered in the register, which may be in book form or on cards. There is no single method of compilation in general use, and many libraries have abolished accession registers altogether. Details recorded include accession number, price, bookseller, branch, date of addition, binding and discard, as well as the usual author, title and publisher. The accession number links the book with the bookseller's invoice and identifies each copy in the catalogue and the issue system. This link between the book and the invoice may also be useful for audit purposes.

A shelf-list is a stock record in classified order, of bookstock at each service point. It may provide a link between the catalogue and the charging system when accession numbers are used for charging. Many libraries do without a shelf-list preferring to rely on the classified catalogue instead.

The main stock record of any library is its catalogues, which are the keys to the library stock, arranged in a recognized order.

Various added entries are included to ease tracing by different approaches. The catalogue records, describes and indexes the resources of a library.

Assignments
1 Describe a procedure for dealing with the receipt of periodicals in a library and claiming any that are overdue. (CGLI 1979)
2 Describe the various processes involved in the acquisition of a new book from the time it has been selected for purchase until it is ready for use by a reader. (CGLI 1980)
3 Explain the purpose of stocktaking and describe the routines and records that are involved in the process. (CGLI 1980)
4 Compile a list of essential statistics that it is considered should be kept in a library, giving a short justification for each item. (CGLI 1971)
5 Describe the following items used in book purchasing procedures:
   – book order form
   – consignment note
   – invoice
   – statement
   When is each used and what is its significance? (CGLI 1970)

Chapter 5

CLASSIFICATION AND CATALOGUING

Classification gathers similar things together, and separates unlike things. Examples of classification are met every day in all kinds of circumstances and books are no exception. There are various classified arrangements for books, depending on different features. Most books are read because of their subject matter, irrespective of their publisher, title or even author, and so a subject arrangement is most useful to readers.

Classification in libraries has several advantages. It arranges books in a helpful order on the shelves, and assists in re-shelving books more easily. It refers quickly from the catalogue to the shelves, and offers a method of clear and effective shelf-guiding. Issues and statistics are often recorded on the basis of the classification scheme in use, and special tasks such as stocktaking are often helped by the classification system. All in all it is a great time saver, and assists in many routine library operations.

It is impossible to arrange subjects so that every relationship is indicated, and detailed subdivision often separates material which might be more usefully shelved together. Several disadvantages such as the changing order of knowledge, and the content and make up of books can seriously affect the usefulness of library classification. Problems, such as the unavoidable disorder of bookshelves and the impracticability of reclassifying large sections of the library also impair effectiveness.

Book classification
There are several special features of a book classification scheme which attempt to assist with problems particular to books. A *generalia* class includes books covering many topics, such as encyclopaedias, and may also include books whose interest lies in their form rather than in their subject content, such as

45

collections and general periodicals. Many classification schemes use a generalia class to tidy up those items which do not fit easily elsewhere. *Form classes* are for books whose main interest lies in the form in which they are written, rather than in the topics which they may be about. Literature is such a class, where, for instance, a play or a poem about coal-mining will be read because it is a play or a poem, and very seldom because it is about coal-mining. *Form divisions* indicate a special way in which a book is written, or an aspect from which a topic is studied. Often, these aspects, such as history, apply to many subjects and common form divisions may be used to describe any topic.

The *notation* is the series of symbols representing the terms of a classification scheme. These symbols provide a convenient shortened reference to the actual class names. The symbols are added to the backs of books to help shelving, and provide a useful link between the catalogue and the shelves. The notation is essential for the practical application of a book classification scheme, and offers many practical advantages. It is used as a short sign on all parts of the book, and in the issue system. It is a guide to the sequence of the classification tables, and enables the use of the index to be made. Clear and efficient guiding of the shelves is made easier, and the efficient use of the catalogues is also helped. The notation may consist of any symbols, letters, figures or arbitary signs and is said to be 'mixed' when two or more kinds of symbols are used, and 'pure' when only one kind is used. Notation may also increase the mnemonic value of a classification scheme. *Mnemonics* are memory aids which are frequently used to indicate certain aspects of a topic, which may be represented by the same symbols whenever they are used. Some classification schemes can indicate form divisions and geographical divisions in the same way each time they occur, and this reduces the need for repetition in the schedules. Mnemonics assist the memory by minimizing reference to the main tables, and are therefore a valuable, but subsidiary, quality of good notation.

For ease of reference, most classification schemes have an *index*, which comprises an alphabetical list of terms, with their corresponding notations. A good index should include all synonyms, and should help to ensure that topics are always classified in the same place. It also assists in finding subjects in the main schedules of the classification scheme, and on the library shelves. Many libraries use the index to a classification scheme as a substitute for a specially compiled subject index of the books in their collection. A *relative index* shows the relation of each subject to other aspects and subjects, so that alternative ways of treating subjects are not overlooked. The notation is provided for each subsidiary heading in a relative index.

Decimal classification

The commonest library classification scheme is the Decimal Classification, devised by an American, Melvil Dewey, in 1876 and now in its nineteenth edition. Because it is American in origin, and also because its original structure and general principles were formulated many years ago, it has many disadvantages for British libraries but it is easily modified to suit local needs and it is very popular, especially amongst public libraries.

The whole of knowledge is divided into nine subject areas, and a generalia class is also added. The ten main classes are:

001-009	Generalities
100-199	Philosophy
200-299	Religion
300-399	Social sciences
400-499	Language
500-599	Pure sciences
600-699	Technology
700-799	The arts
800-899	Literature
900-999	Geography and history

Each main class has ten divisions, each division has ten subdivisions, and so on. Subjects with more than ten subdivisions usually have minor topics grouped together at number nine as 'others'. Throughout the schedules, practical usefulness has been given prior consideration over theory, and this has helped to make the scheme so popular.

Many critics complain of the illogical arrangement of classes and subdivisions, and of the artificiality of many divisions. Some of the arrangement is out of date, and there can be delay in the publication of revised editions of the schedules, leaving no places for important new subjects. Average classification numbers tend to be longer, and the American bias and terminology can cause problems. The scheme is of little value in special libraries. On the credit side, it is relatively simple, easily understood, used and remembered. It is flexible and easily modified. It can be applied to material of all kinds, and is available in convenient printed form. An organization which ensures its permanent revision has been established for several years now. So many libraries use it that it has become almost the universal public library scheme. Its adoption by the *British national bibliography*, and its easy assimilation into computerized systems, has ensured its place as the most widely used scheme, despite the many faults which it may possess.

Other classification schemes

The *Universal Decimal Classification* (UDC) is a very detailed classification scheme often used in special libraries. It is based on Dewey's Decimal Classification and retains this order and character in outline, although there are many other differences. There is no three figure minimum notation, so that main subjects can be represented by one or two digits only (e.g. Applied Science 6, Engineering 62). Where there are larger numbers decimal points are used to divide at three digit intervals (e.g. Radar 621.396.96). Several arbitrary signs (e.g. + / :) are introduced to indicate relationships, and there are tables of special subdivision to indicate form, place, time, language and other aspects. This mixture of signs, numbers and sometimes letters can give very detailed and complex placings, but the notation may become quite cumbersome. UDC is published and kept up to date by the British Standards Institution, in Britain, and one advantage is that Dewey's American bias is therefore not reflected in the terminology or structure.

The *Colon Classification*, first published in 1933, was devised by Dr S Ranganathan and adopted a new approach to library classification. The scheme is not a list of subjects or topics in a pre-arranged order, but instead it enables class numbers to be constructed by adding components from different schedules, using arbitrary signs as links and indicators. Ranganathan claimed that a suitable classification number could be built up in this way for any topic, however complex. The Colon classification is not used in a large public library in Britain, but its theories have had widespread influence on many special subject schemes such as the

London Education Classification and the sfB Building Classification.

The *Library of Congress Classification* began as a special scheme to meet the particular requirements of the Library of Congress, which houses a vast collection with many special problems. The classification scheme was not devised with any particular theory in mind, but rather with the contents of the Library and patterns of usage foremost. This arrangement of grouping according to the ways in which the literature of a subject tends to be structured and used by writers and scholars is sometimes called 'literary warrant'. In practice, each main subject is completely separate, with an individual framework and its own index. The main classes and subdivisions use an alphabetical notation, and further subdivisions are numerical. This gives a lengthy, mixed notation which can be difficult to remember and to use. There is no general index. The scheme is effective and generally works well, but it is too complex to be used widely in British public libraries, although some university libraries use it. The schedules are revised promptly, and uniformity is ensured by the use of printed cards and MARC tapes produced by the cooperative cataloguing division at the Library of Congress.

The *Bibliographic Classification* was first published by Bliss in 1935, and a revised edition has begun to appear recently. It is arranged in a scholarly and logical way generally accepted by academics as being the way in which subjects are taught and practised. Subjects are developed from the general to the particular, and related subjects like science and technology are arranged together. There is provision for alternative placings, but this adaptability can also be confusing and lead to inconsistencies. Auxiliary tables are provided for compound subjects, and spaces are left for new subjects to be inserted. The notation is mainly alphabetical. There are simple form divisions and a good relative index. Revisions to the schedules are announced regularly in the Bliss Bulletin.

Practical classification
Broad classification is a term used to indicate the use of the main sections of a classification scheme to minimize the complexity for readers. It may be introduced in a small library or, especially, in a children's library. It offers the advantage of shorter classification

numbers, and it can also be expanded as the collection grows.

In many libraries, novels and light fiction are taken out of Dewey sequence and are filed alphabetically by authors' surnames. Often quick reference books are shelved in a convenient, separate sequence. Music scores and other categories of special material such as oversize books may also be shelved on the bottom shelf of each appropriate tier, or in a separate sequence altogether. These provisions for oversize books are known as *parallel arrangements*, and any alteration of the normal sequence of books is called *broken order*. Any variation in the general shelving pattern should be indicated to the reader via the catalogue.

Catalogues

A library catalogue is a list of books and other material housed in that library, with entries arranged in a recognized order, containing information about each book or other item. It gives the reader an overall view of the entire bookstock, or those sections of it which are required. It is the key to the whole stock of a library, a locating device and an indispensable staff tool.

Most British libraries construct *classified catalogues* in which entries are arranged by their subject classification numbers, so that entries for books on the same subject will be found together and will be beside entries on related topics. Because the main catalogue is in subject number order, two indexes are needed to help readers locate the items they require.

The *subject index* is an alphabetical index of subjects showing the classification numbers assigned to each subject. The *author index* has entries arranged in alphabetical order of authors' surnames. To find out what books the library has on any subject, the reader must first consult the subject index to find the classification number for that subject. Then the reader must consult the classification number in the catalogue or go straight to the shelves to see what is immediately available on that topic. To find out whether the library has a book by a certain author, the reader should consult the author index, and this again will refer the reader to the classified catalogue, if additional details are required.

A *dictionary catalogue* lists entries under headings arranged in alphabetical sequence. Specific subject headings are chosen, and the reader is directed from one subject to another by an elaborate system of 'see' and 'see also' references. Some dictionary catalogues have separate author and subject sequences, but most are filed together alphabetically. The range of material that a library holds is not immediately apparent, since related topics are filed by the accident of their alphabetical titles. Many readers seem more familiar with the alphabetical arrangement, which can also show titles in addition to subjects.

Cataloguing rules
Whichever type of catalogue is used, each book will have a main entry which lists the book under name of the author, or body responsible for its creation, together with full bibliographical details (see Figure 2). There is only one main entry, but there may be many added entries for joint authors and other subordinates, e.g. editors, translators, series.

The main entry is usually divided into five parts, viz:

1 Heading – this is usually the name of the author or body responsible for producing the book.

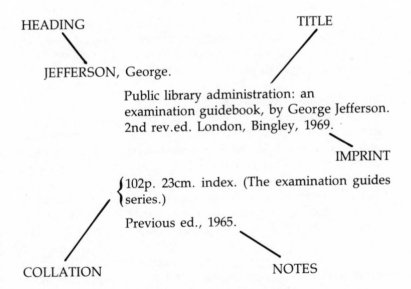

HEADING

TITLE

JEFFERSON, George.

Public library administration: an
examination guidebook, by George Jefferson.
2nd rev.ed. London, Bingley, 1969.

IMPRINT

{102p. 23cm. index. (The examination guides
series.)

Previous ed., 1965.

COLLATION

NOTES

Figure 2: The five parts of a catalogue main entry

2 Title – this is written as it appears on the title page. It includes the name of the author, or editor, and also the number of the edition, other than the first.

3 Imprint – this comprises the place of publication, the publisher and the date.

4 Collation – this is the physical description of the book, including the number of volumes, pages, illustrations, size and series, if any.

5 Notes – these are bibliographical notes concerning, for example, the publishing history of the book, and should not be confused with the annotation which refers to the contents of the books, or its intended readership.

Rules are laid down to ensure accuracy and consistency when cataloguing. The cataloguing rules are collected into codes, of which several exist. A revised second edition of the Anglo-American Cataloguing Rules appeared in 1978, widely referred to as AACR2. The new edition continues to follow the same principles and underlying objectives of the first edition, and extends the coverage to include the consideration of computerized cataloguing, the increase in centralized and cooperative cataloguing, and the newer types of audio-visual and other library materials. The rules are intended to give guidance on a comprehensive range of possible headings and entries, and as such provide a detailed and complex set of examples, which are extremely valuable to practising cataloguers.

Physical forms of catalogue

Library catalogues were once frequently produced in *printed book* form. This is the quickest and easiest form of catalogue to consult, but it is uneconomic to produce, and soon becomes out of date. Entries cannot easily be added, and there is very little flexibility. Printed catalogues were quite popular when library bookstocks were more static, or perhaps organized on closed access, and there are still some fine examples produced for special collections.

The *guard book* was compiled on the scrap book principle. The flexibility of the printed catalogue was improved by leaving spaces or inserting extra pages when required. Although this was a partial solution, maintenance was still difficult, and additional copies were needed while the others were updated.

Sheaf catalogues carry separate paper entries in loose-leaf binders, which can be taken to the shelves, when consulted. Unfortunately, they can also be lost. They offer complete flexibility, but are slow to use. They can be stored in a variety of ways, since they can be brought to reading height when in use. Entries can be duplicated by typewriter, using carbons.

Card entries are filed in drawers, housed in cabinets. These are simple to maintain, but take up considerable space, since they must remain at reading height and can only expand sideways. Readers often complain about congestion at card cabinets, since one user effectively prevents another from using all the immediately adjacent catalogue drawers. Solutions to this problem have been tried by spacing drawers more widely, or by allowing access from the front or back simultaneously, but the problem remains largely unsolved.

The main problems arise from the dual use of catalogues. The librarian, especially the cataloguer, needs a flexible catalogue which can accommodate additions and withdrawals easily, at any time. Readers are primarily concerned with quick and easy consultation, regardless of whether someone else may be using it also.

Where *computer catalogues* are used, they are often produced in microfilm form, either in cassettes or on microfiche. Although they are extremely efficient to produce and amend, they must be consulted by means of microreading machines. The problem of congestion among readers still remains, and some readers are reluctant to use them. One big advantage is that copies can be cheaply produced, giving small libraries access to the complete stock of larger library systems. They are kept up-to-date by supplements, and these can prove wearisome to use, particularly if fully revised, updated versions are issued infrequently.

Some libraries with computer catalogues are experimenting with public access online systems, which enable readers to consult catalogue records from live computer terminals. This facility may also enable readers to check their own issue records and reserve books for themselves. As computer systems become more user friendly, and equipment more readily and cheaply available, such improvements and developments will become more widespread.

Centralized cataloguing is carried out by a central library or organization so that all member libraries may share the cataloguing therefore avoiding duplication of effort, and providing a uniform standard entry. The British Library Bibliographic Services Division produces MARC computer tapes, which are a machine readable version of the BNB and Library of Congress bibliographic records. Subscribing libraries use the MARC tapes to produce local catalogues with their own computers, or a complete catalogue service can be provided to meet the requirements of individual libraries. Cooperative networks can be established to create a central computer database which other libraries can also use. An obvious example of such a network is the Birmingham Libraries Cooperative Mechanization Project (BLCMP), which provides a cataloguing service for subscribing libraries, and has taken over the production of printed catalogue cards previously issued by the British National Bibliography. Since 1977 a computer system known as BLAISE (British Library Automated Information Service) has facilitated general library housekeeping routines from catalogue production to bibliographic checking, and cooperates in the production of *Books in English*.

A union catalogue is the combined catalogue of the bookstocks of various libraries or branches. It makes the total book resources of an area available for consultation by everyone in that area, and provides book locations.

Catalogue filing
Before any filing is done, it is essential to discover which method of filing is used; whether it is the 'letter by letter' also known as the 'all through' method, or the 'word by word' sometimes called the 'nothing before something' method.

'Letter by letter' means that word formation on the card heading should be ignored. Each letter as it follows the next is considered for its place in the alphabet, and for no other reason. For 'word by word' filing, each word is taken as it appears, using the same strict letter order, but in this case stopping at the end of each word.

The following example, taken from a section of a subject index relating to books on all aspects of children, illustrates clearly just how much difference is made in an alphabetical order when one method is chosen rather than the other. It also shows the necessity for ensuring that one single filing method is followed consistently at all times, by every member of staff.

Letter by letter	*Word by word*
child allowances	child allowances
childbirth	child guidance
child guidance	child psychology
childhood diseases	child welfare
childkilling	childbirth
child psychology	childhood diseases
children in care	childkilling
children's games	children in care
children's literature	children's games
child welfare	children's literature

Withdrawal and disposal

Catalogues must be constantly revised to ensure accuracy and consistency. Much ephemeral material is best left uncatalogued and is therefore easy to discard, e.g. travel information and careers literature. Often, where the relevance of material is uncertain, an intermediate step, such as relegation to a stack or reserve collection, can be introduced, provided that catalogue entries are suitably amended. New editions will almost certainly render older copies obsolete. These may be discarded or circulated to branch libraries where bookstocks may be less representative.

On withdrawal, all relevant records should be amended or discarded, as appropriate. Withdrawals should be notified to headquarters sections, for union catalogue amendments and some items may be offered to subject specialist libraries. Some libraries offer older material to their readers for sale. Most discarded material is mutilated or destroyed to prevent unauthorized resale elsewhere. All discards should be clearly marked, statistics kept and stock records altered accordingly.

Assignments

1 Describe the main features of a book classification scheme known to you, explaining its particular strengths and weaknesses. (CGLI 1987)
2 In a classification scheme, what is meant by each of the following:
   a mixed notation
   b relative index
   c mnemonics

d form classes?
(CGLI 1980)
3 Give *four* reasons why books are sometimes arranged out of sequence in a library. State the advantages and disadvantages of such arrangements. (CGLI 1978)
4 Outline the characteristics of *two* of the following types of catalogue, and describe the advantages and disadvantages of *each*:
a card catalogue
b fiche catalogue
c online catalogue
(CGLI 1986)
5 (a) Name the separate parts into which the main entry in a library catalogue is divided.
(b) Make up and set out an example of a main entry. (CGLI 1981)

Chapter 6

NON-BOOK MATERIAL

Non-book material is generally understood to be any resource material which is not in the form of a printed book. Thus a range of non-book materials would include the following items: cassette tapes, charts, computer tapes, filmstrips, film loops, films, journals, magazines, maps, microfiche, microfilm, newspapers, newspaper cuttings, pamphlets, periodicals, photographs, records, slides, video tapes.

The term 'non-book materials' thus covers material of both the printed and audio-visual kinds. Audio-visual resources are designed to transmit information either by sound or by vision, and as such are library resources which do not depend on the printed word in order to make communication with their users. Since however, the term 'non-book material' does include such printed items as pamphlets and newspapers, it becomes clear that although all audio-visual materials can be considered to be non-book materials, not all non-book materials are audio-visual materials.

Rapid technological developments have caused librarians to reassess their library stock provision in the light of the demands and needs of borrowers living and working in the second half of the twentieth century. The need for the swift transmission of information in the fields of industry and commerce has resulted in the creation of a wide range of communication media other than books, computerized, teletext, viewdata and the like. Similarly within the home itself we all surround ourselves with a range of media such as television, radio and sound and video recorders which communicate in other ways than by the printed word. At the same time changes in the world of education have prompted increased individualized learning and information seeking on the part of school children and students alike. These are three of the main factors which have resulted in librarians acquiring a varied collection of non-book materials to supplement their traditional bookstock. The majority of libraries have added such new material to their shelves gradually, firstly in response to the needs of their borrowers, secondly in relation to the space and housing facilities available, and thirdly according to the money available. The gradual acquisition of new types of material has given library staff time to assess realistically the possibilities and problems associated with the acquisition and growth of non-book collections. One main advantage of a library providing such material is that much more up-to-date information on many subjects is carried. Another advantage is that it is much easier to discard material not in book form when it becomes out of date or otherwise obsolete. In order that the fullest possible use is made of this less traditional library material, it is essential that all members of a library staff should familiarize themselves with the materials available in their particular library. There will be opportunity to do so if and when they are required to assist in their processing, their lettering and labelling, or in their reinforcing. Once the material has been acquired, an overall strategy has to be devised concerning its handling in relation to its classification and cataloguing, its location and its storage.

Classification and cataloguing
The overwhelming majority of libraries in this country use the Dewey Decimal Classification system for their bookstock arrangement, incorporating this system into a centralized classified catalogue. No one such near universal system has yet emerged in relation to the classification and cataloguing of non-book materials, although the need for one is now fully acknowledged. A number of associations, namely the Anglo-American Cataloguing Rules (AACR), Association of Special Library and Information Bureaux (ASLIB) and Council for Educational Technology for the United Kingdom (CET) are working on the formulation of overall policies relating to the cataloguing of non-book media. Meanwhile some libraries have opted to use a modified adaptation of the Dewey system in conjunction with their main central catalogue, but others have elected to catalogue non-book materials quite independently of bookstock, using one or other of the schemes known as 'coordinate indexing'. Yet other

libraries have dispensed with any classification at all in relation to non-book materials, choosing to arrange the latter in chronological order within their respective formats of films, records, tapes etc.

Libraries which have chosen to classify and catalogue non-book stock by using Dewey classification and a centralized catalogue, argue that this is the most logical way to indicate the library's coverage of a particular subject, irrespective of the format of the information supplied on that subject. Also it is felt that the interrelationships between books and other materials are best demonstrated by the use of one single centralized catalogue. Non-book items are classified according to Dewey and given a main entry in the catalogue. On the catalogue card is a reference indicating where a particular item is to be found, e.g.

Location . . . . . . record collection

Some libraries attempt to extend their demonstration of interrelationships to the actual shelving of materials, so that records and cassettes of music, say, are shelved in the same sequence as books written about music. Since few libraries have sufficient space for housing such varying media together, this unified shelving arrangement is unlikely to be practised on a large scale. Other libraries instead of having a main entry in their catalogue for each non-book item, make use of the subject index card to indicate all the non-book materials which are available in connection with one particular subject. (See Figure 3.)

Other libraries are in favour of cutting the cataloguing of non-book material down to the barest minimum, arguing that the simpler the system, the more willingly and more frequently it will be used by borrowers. Another factor relating to a simple system is that it ensures that less staff time is spent on both the processing and the discarding of material. Chronological ordering of material involves giving each non-book item an accession number as it becomes a part of library stock. Each accession number is then prefaced by a letter or letters, which indicate the type or format of the particular non-book item. Thus a library already holding 400 non-book items acquires a filmstrip on, say, the Sahara desert. The strip is given the accession number 401, and this is prefaced by FS, indicating that it will be found in the filmstrip collection. Adjacent to the filmstrip collection a list will be displayed *front of card*

Aeroplanes			629.13
Books	*	Filmstrips	*
Cassettes		Slides	*
Records		Photographs	*

back of card

Books	629.13	Filmstrips	F 39
		Slides	SL 32-40
		Photographs	P 81-99

Figure 3: A sample subject index card for retrieving information from a range of library materials

which indicates the subject matter of each film strip:

Filmstrips collection
FS 49 domestic animals (cats)
FS 62 steam engines
FS 88 Chester Zoo

FS 105 kite making
FS 209 canal navigation
FS 401 Sahara desert

The staff of smaller libraries are devising a variety of short-term and small-scale solutions to the problems of recording audio-visual material. In the long term, however, it is clear that audio-visual materials are representing a major and increasing part of the national and world output and heritage of recorded knowledge, and they should receive equivalent treatment with that of printed material. As long ago as 1974, there was a joint British Library/Council of Education Technology study on the need for a national cataloguing and information service for audio-visual materials, which recognized that a wide range of non-print resources existed, but that the lack of central reference and cataloguing services hindered efficient access to them. To create a total system in one step was considered impossible, but a start has been made with a manageable amount of material of particular interest to libraries in all types of institutions (see Chapter 9, page 91). The British Library is now involved in the collection, recording and preservation of audio-visual materials and close cooperation between major bodies including notably CET, ASLIB and the LA is now being actively pursued with the provision of centralized and cooperative AV cataloguing services.

Location of non-book materials
The first major question to be decided concerning the placing of non-book materials is whether they will be on open or closed access: i.e. whether they are to be put in the public part of the library, to be handled at will by borrowers, or whether they are to be stored in rooms to which only the library staff have access. This decision is usually dictated by the format of the non-book item in question. It can easily be seen that both methods have their advantages and their disadvantages.

The advantages of open access tend to favour the potential borrower. Placed in the main part of the library, non-book items are much more likely to catch the attention of library members, and for that reason alone, are much more likely to be readily used. Open access also facilitates the examination of the items, and enables borrowers to browse amongst them. On the other hand, displayed items are more likely to 'disappear' and to become damaged by being more frequently handled.

Closed access enables librarians to store materials in a much more economical way, since items do not have to be displayed for the public. Rooms without windows can be used, and no circulation space for borrowers is required. There is also less potential damage liable to stock. But to store material on closed access does mean that a higher percentage of staff time is spent on retrieving items for borrowers. It also means that more time has to be spent on the library's cataloguing system, if borrowers are to be kept fully informed of all that is available for loan. Generally speaking, more libraries seem to be moving towards open access for non-book materials, as audio-visual material in particular becomes increasingly available and more cheaply produced.

Storage of non-book materials
Too much direct heat, from radiators for example, causes items such as records to warp, whilst strong sunlight can play havoc with items made from paper, even to the extent of constituting a fire risk. The dust contained in the atmosphere and the humidity of a particular environment are factors to be taken into consideration before certain items are housed. Both open and closed access locations need to be carefully vetted for any possible damage to materials. The rest of this chapter will be concerned with the storage requirements of particular types of materials, each of which require their own special considerations.

Slides
Slides can now be housed in commercially produced slide boxes, each slide having its own individual slot into which it fits. Or if they are going to be viewed in the library building itself, slides can be kept in slide trays ready for immediate transfer to the library's projector. These two methods of storage are only appropriate if the slides are to be shown as a whole set. When preliminary viewing of slides is required, for a selection of slides to be made, it is essential that slides are stored in such a way that they can easily be inspected. In this case, slides are best housed in transparent plastic wallets, with a separate pocket for each slide, and each wallet holding 20 or more slides. These wallets

are then stored in ordinary filing cabinets suspended by a metal attachment which runs along the whole length of the top edge of the wallet. By holding such a wallet in front of a light or a window, the user is then able to examine its contents without needing to handle each slide separately. Similar see-through wallets, though somewhat smaller and holding around 12 slides, can be placed in ring binders. The whole unit then resembles the form of a book, and can be shelved vertically like the bookstock.

To house very large collections comprising hundreds of slides, special purpose-built cabinets are available. The cabinets are in three sections. In the left and right hand sections the slides are held in a series of movable panels. The middle section consists of a viewing panel with its own built in light source. When slides need inspecting the appropriate panel is pushed across until it is in front of the illuminated viewing panel.

Newspaper cuttings
The ways in which a library stores its newspaper cuttings are dictated by the purpose of its collections and also by the length of time for which they will be required. A collection of cuttings on a topical subject such as a Royal Wedding, which is likely to be quickly outdated and therefore discarded, can be housed in a box file. The title of the subject of the cuttings is entered on the outside of the box file. As each cutting is acquired the name of its source, i.e. that of the newspaper or magazine, along with its date are written at the top of the cutting which is then simply added to the existing contents of the file box.

Cuttings intended to form a more permanent collection are mounted on to thin cardboard of uniform size, supplied at the top with a uniform heading consisting of topic title, name of its source, and the date, and deposited in a filing cabinet. Here the cuttings will be arranged in the order considered most appropriate, which may be chronological or under different aspects of the topic.

Some cuttings collections lend themselves to being housed in a scrap book, each cutting simply being pasted into the book on its arrival. Alternatively, if the collection is going to become a permanent item of library stock, the cuttings can be kept loose until the total collection has been acquired, and then arranged systematically into the scrap book. Pasting cuttings on to the single sheets of a loose-leaf binder is a useful way of ensuring the flexibility of a collection. Such a collection can be updated, withdrawn from or reshaped, as the need arises.

Maps and charts

The type of storage used for these items is largely dictated by the amount of money available. The cheapest method undoubtedly is to have the map or chart rolled up, with one of its open ends visible, and either stacked on a shelf or fitted into a rack resembling an umbrella stand. The end of the map can have a tag dangling from it to indicate its subject matter. If money is available, however, it is more satisfactory to provide a set of shallow drawers known as a map chest, which enables maps to be stored flat and consequently to be more easily used.

The most effective way of map and chart storage is achieved by some form of suspension since this enables the items to be examined instantaneously. There are sets of wall mounted arms available which grip a set of maps or charts. These arms are pivoted so that the user is able to browse through the entire collection, and even detach one item if he wishes to examine it more closely on a flat surface. Alternatively, maps can be held by large bulldog clips, which can be threaded on to a rod so that the maps are suspended, making them easier to consult.

Whatever the storage method adopted by a particular library, constant care has to be taken to ensure a longer life for the inevitably fragile collections of maps and charts. Some libraries are now taking slide photographs of their charts, so that borrowers can examine the scope of the collection without the actual charts being handled. Libraries are beginning to invest in seal presses which facilitate the reinforcing of maps and charts by laminating and backing them with strong transparent film.

Film

Film items, whatever their format, usually arrive in the containers supplied by the manufacturers, and these units in their turn are best housed in fireproof metal cabinets. It is important that the manufacturer's instructions regarding the storage of these items are strictly complied with, in order both to prevent deterioration in their condition and also to prevent their being destroyed by fire.

Filmstrips
These come in small cylindrical boxes, the top of each bearing a circular label indicating the contents of the box. After each has had an accession number added to its label it is stored with others in a shallow metal drawer which forms part of a cabinet. If no more than 20 filmstrips are housed in each drawer the particular number of box required can be quickly identified. It is essential that adjacent to the cabinet is placed a list of all the filmstrips' titles. The list can be simply in the form of a typewritten sheet reinforced with thin cardboard. If, however, the collection is being constantly revised and supplemented, the provision of a visible index, which allows for each new title to be inserted on its own separate cardboard strip, does away with the necessity of retyping whole lists of items.

Microfilm
The problems associated with the storing and retrieving of old newspapers are known to everyone who has ever had to handle these items. The older the newspapers, the more brittle they become. The more they are subjected to sunlight and to artificial light, the more quickly their sheets become yellow, and their print becomes faded. As far as their handling goes, even to attempt to withdraw a newspaper from under a large pile of others is difficult. For these reasons, as well as in the interests of cutting down on storage space required for newspapers, many of the larger libraries are ordering microfilm copies of newspapers. Each microfilm consists of a continuous roll of film on which is recorded one month's issues of any one daily newspaper, and this is kept in a cardboard box. Upended, the cardboard boxes, each labelled with the title of the newspaper, the month and the year of the particular issues, are stored in sliding drawers within strong metal cabinets. Microfilm readers, which project a magnified image of the microfilm on to a screen, are made available in the library itself, so that the intending reader is able to locate and study for himself the particular newspaper item which interests him.

Microfiche
This is not usually a lending item. It is a type of microform which is being increasingly used for the presentation of a wide variety of information. Many library catalogues are now in this form, as

are union catalogues of various kinds. *Whitaker's books in print* can now be purchased in microfiche form, the individual fiches being fitted into a hardbacked ring file and handled like a book. Magazines and journals can be ordered in microfiche form, the whole of one issue of a journal appearing on a piece of microfiche roughly the size of a postcard. Each microfiche is placed in its own separate pocket type envelope so that the heading of each is clearly visible. Yearly indexes to the articles contained in the journals, also in microfiche, are filed in their appropriate place, and all are housed in metal drawers/cabinets.

Computer software
Computer software may be audio cassettes or floppy discs, and these items should be stored away from radiators and windows since direct heat or sunlight could corrupt the package. Since not all software runs on every type or model of computer, the software needs to be arranged according to the hardware required, so that users will not select incompatible programmes. Most educational software is prepared for use on BBC microcomputers, but there may even be incompatibility between different BBC models, and this can be irritating for users, and may also create other problems such as hardware malfunction.

Records
Ideally, record collections are best made available to be browsed over by the intending borrower. Library equipment manufacturers sell record browser boxes which will hold and support records in such a way that the front of the first record and of each subsequent one as the first record is moved forward, is in full view. Some libraries, wanting to encourage browsing yet also wishing to prolong the life of their records, have only the commercial sleeve available in the browser box. The record itself is kept in closed access, housed in a plain cardboard sleeve on which is recorded the disc's identification and location.

When large numbers of records are to be made accessible to the public, an open fronted cupboard or box enables a number of records to be stood on end and placed in a row. Wooden struts are placed at short intervals along the length of the cupboard or box. In this way no more than half a dozen or so records are held together in any one section. This facilitates examination of the records; it also helps to prevent the records from becoming warped or their sleeves from sticking to one another.

It is best if similar sized records are housed together in one sequence, and separated from records of a different size. Otherwise smaller records get lost behind larger ones, and there is more likelihood of damage occurring. It is quite safe to leave a pile of the smallest sized records flat for browsing purposes, but not so the larger ones. The latter should always be stacked in a vertical position.

In spite of all the precautions taken to preserve records, they are still amongst the most vulnerable items of a library's stock, not least when out on loan. Some libraries do not allow records to be lent until the stylus of the record player on which they are to be played has been brought to the library for inspection. More libraries, in particular the specialist ones with large record collections, are choosing to produce their own cassette tapes from their records, and to make these, rather than the records themselves, available for loan. This can only be done under licence and according to the rules of the Mechanical Copyright Protection Society.

Since browsers' requirements in relation to records are usually most specific, much care and thought has to be given to the arrangement of records within a library's collection. It is usual to arrange classical music records in alphabetical order by composer. Non-classical music is divided into categories such as pop, jazz, progressive, brass and arranged in alphabetical order by artist; whilst spoken word items are arranged alphabetically by author or artist as appropriate.

Assignments

1 List the non-book materials found in the library where you work, and discuss their advantages and disadvantages compared with books and journals. (CGLI 1987)
2 Discuss the main advantages and disadvantages associated with
   a open access storage of non-book materials and
   b closed access storage of non-book materials.
3 Methods of storing non-book materials are largely dictated by costs. From the following list of materials, suggest ways of storing each in a small primary school library and in a large central public library:

a maps and charts
b colour slides
c newspaper cuttings
d records

Chapter 7

GOOD HOUSEKEEPING

One of the aims of staff working in any type of library, be it public, educational, or special, should be to ensure that the right book or right information is produced as speedily as possible after a request has been received from the borrower. It is essential therefore for library staff to be both energetic and accurate in their service, to avoid wasting both the enquirer's time and the library's.

As all workers in libraries know to their cost, one of the main factors causing delay is the 'lost' book. So often when a book is missing from its rightful place on the shelves it is inaccurate to term it a 'lost' book. It may have been sent for rebinding, withdrawn for repairs, put on one side because it is reserved or required for inter-library loan; or it could simply be missing through having been wrongly shelved.

Good housekeeping ensures that the incidence of lost and missing books is kept to a minimum. After a returned book has been discharged, and before it is put on the trolley for re-shelving, it should be briefly inspected for any minor repair requirements, any recent damage and to see if the date label requires renewing. Not least this quick flip through of the pages can reveal bookmarks, orthodox or otherwise. The observant assistant must also be on the lookout for any notes or signs attached to the bookcard, which may indicate that a particular book should be retained at the counter because there is a waiting list for it, or because it has been requested on inter-library loan.

Shelving
The assistant is now ready to deal with the majority of the day's returned books that are ready to go back into circulation. Some libraries leave their main shelving until borrowers are out of the

way, others wait for a slack period before starting to shelve, whilst yet others work strictly on a 'shelving every hour' basis, however busy the library traffic happens to be. But in all these cases the first task is to sort the books into categories, e.g. fiction, non-fiction, oversize, out of sequence; the second task is to arrange each category of books into the exact order in which they will appear on their respective shelves. If possible it should be arranged so that the books can all be disposed of in one circular trip round the library. It is worth noting that efficient shelving is only achieved when the library assistant is thoroughly familiar with the shelf arrangement and with any 'exceptions to the rule' which might appertain in his or her own particular library, e.g. the language (400) and the literature (800) Dewey main classes are often located on adjacent shelves to suit the borrowers' convenience.

A new assistant would be well advised to spend some time coming to terms with the stock and its location before shelving an armful or a trolley full of books. Not all libraries use trolleys as an aid to shelving, and if assistants' arms are the accepted substitute for trolleys, it is worth taking care over the quantity of books that can be conveniently carried on one arm, and making sure that the other arm is left completely free to perform the actual process of getting the books on to the shelves. Sometimes before starting the actual shelving it may be necessary to rearrange the shelves, loosening books in order to insert further books with ease, otherwise a book can be so firmly jammed into its correct position that it becomes difficult at some future stage to separate one plastic jacketed book from another. The art lies in loosening a shelf of books sufficiently for it to take a couple of extra books if and when necessary, without leaving a yawning gap; which tempts a borrower to deposit a book there, appropriately or otherwise! Or, if the practice in your library is to leave space at the end of each shelf for returned stock, inserting a book end or slanting the last book at an angle will similarly remove the temptation for the borrower to fill those spaces. Another point worth noting is that the appearance of books is neater if they are straightened so as to be level with the front edge of the shelves. By doing this, differences in book sizes become less obvious, and the resulting uniformity helps to maintain the tidy appearance of the library.

In addition to the routine shelving sessions, good housekeeping demands that books and other printed materials are sorted through at regular intervals and checked that they are in correct order. At the same time a check should be made on the visibility of the titles of works and of labels indicating classification numbers and so on, since with time the latter often become mutilated or illegible. Not only does regular renewal of labels help in the general good appearance of the library; it also helps to ensure that non-fiction books are shelved at their correct place in the classification scheme. Non-fiction books should always be arranged according to the first three letters of the authors' name within each class sequence.

Apart from the one example of the exception to the rule book sequence already mentioned, there are in the majority of libraries several other examples of these special categories to be noted by the library assistant. Usually each category has its own special symbol or code, which is added to the catalogue entry of the book and also very often to the class number on the spine of the book itself. The symbols (R) and (p) indicate that reference books and pamphlets respectively are housed in special areas away from the normal book sequence, whilst OS (or even f for folio size) indicates an oversize book which will be found among other such books on a wider shelf, very often the bottom shelf of a stack.

Large public libraries have built up in the past their own specialist collections as a contribution to the inter-library lending system. Because of the size of such collections they too are often treated as out-of-sequence books since they are housed separately from the main sequence of the particular library's non-fiction stock, this being indicated on the catalogue entry. Similarly, lack of space often prevents the displaying of all stock on open shelves, and little used books have to be labelled (IS) for example, to indicate they are 'in store', and that they will only be produced from the storeroom on request. Most types of libraries, including both public and special, tend to arrange displays of various kinds from time to time; thus stock is temporarily removed from its normal sequence on the shelves, and placed in the display area. Since this can result in 'missing' books as far as the regular user of a particular subject area is concerned, some libraries consider it worthwhile to place dummy books carrying the appropriate titles, in the place of the 'missing' ones.

Non-book materials are yet further examples of items not housed in the normal book sequence. Cataloguing arrangements for materials such as newspaper cuttings, records, cassettes, tapes and slides are various.

Some libraries carry a separate catalogue for each type of such audio-visual materials. But it is also necessary to draw the attention of borrowers to the different types of media available. Many libraries place examples of non-book materials in a prominent position on the wall or at the counter. Displayed record sleeves, for example, can indicate the existence of a library's record collection, and also have the additional effect of brightening up plain walls and dark corners.

Shelf guiding

The decision concerning the type of shelf guiding to be used in a library will have been taken by the librarian, but the maintenance of the good order of those guides will depend on the keen eye of the efficient library assistant. The term 'shelf guiding' covers a wide variety of types of printed headings. These range from the very general, which aid in the locating of the broad categories of books, to the very specific, which, attached to the edge of a shelf, indicate the contents of that particular shelf or part of the shelf. The general headings can be executed in a variety of ways; some libraries use stencilled letters painted on wooden strips, other use cut-out polystyrene, metal or plastic foam letters which give a three-dimensional effect, whilst others have their headings painted directly on to the wall immediately above the appropriate shelves. The more specific guides usually consist of metal or plastic holders into which cardboard strips can be inserted behind a clear perspex protective covering. Some libraries use a typewriter for their cardboard strips; others make their own punched strips with the aid of a machine such as the widely used Dymo. If the latter is used, the strips can be stuck directly on to the shelves, and do not need to be slotted into a holder. Whatever techniques are used in the making of headings, it is helpful if the library assistant, who inevitably makes frequent and regular journeys round the shelves, can quickly spot any deterioration in the condition of the guiding, and put any necessary repairs into operation.

Minor repairs

Repairing minor damage to books is also a part of good housekeeping. A variety of repair material is available and an interested worker can find satisfaction in developing skills appropriate to the task in hand. There are a number of branded transparent tapes which can be used for torn pages, maps and documents. The majority of these do not colour or contract with age; they are therefore quite permanent, and can be written on, using pen or pencil. Coloured tape is available for the edge binding of book covers, maps and pictures, for extra protection, and these tapes can be applied with the aid of an edgebinding machine. Adhesive waterproof tape of varying widths for protecting and reinforcing the spines of books can also be bought – one inch wide for paperbacks and up to three inches wide for use with thicker volumes. Glue can be used for the replacing of pages which are not stitched, but extremely sparing use of it is advised. There are proprietory brands of cleaning fluids available for dissolving dirt on plastic jackets, but surgical spirit performs this action very well, and has the added advantage that there is no associated smell. For the cleaning of pages and illustrations, a piece of putty and a large soft rubber can be useful allies. Soap and water, used gently and sparingly can also play their part. There is a dissolving fluid on the market which copes with the irritating and constantly recurring defacement of pages with biro pens.

When all possible steps have been taken to eradicate the effects of damage, a book may still have to be put back into circulation with its damage still apparent. In this case it is very important that a note should be made of the type of damage and its location in the book, so that succeeding borrowers of the book are not wrongly accused of the offence. The top of the date label at the front of the book would be an appropriate place for such a note to be made.

Book display

Nothing enhances the neat, orderly appearance of a well organized library more than colourful eye-catching displays of books and other materials. These can help to break the monotony of an essentially angular uniformity induced by rectangular shelf units, furniture and books alike and especially if the displays are framed by tastefully arranged plants, dried flower arrangements or ceramics. It is not necessary to have great artistic talents at one's disposal in order to mount a display; nor is it necessary to spend days in the preparation of one. The aim is to choose a topical or otherwise appropriate theme, and to express that theme in such an original way that the reader's attention is caught.

Once the theme has been decided upon, it can be discussed amongst a group of staff members, and this can lead to a fruitful generating of ideas. Notes of these should be immediately jotted down and then an initial sketch or plan drawn to incorporate those considered appropriate. In addition to books and other printed material a good display can be augmented by such items as photographs, cuttings, charts and models. Approaches to the art and craft departments of schools and colleges and to a group such as a local photographic society, can result in excellent items being offered on loan for display purposes. Posters advertised in the press can be obtained, and much useful and colourful background material acquired from travel bureaux or foreign embassies. Free material such as trade handouts can also serve as an invaluable aid in display work. Cut out pictures from plant and flower catalogues, for example, can provide a colourful collage as a background for a display on gardening.

The task of mounting a background for a display is made very much easier if pegboard is available in the library. Commercially marketed hooks, stands, slips etc. can be bought which enable a variety of display material to be fastened to the pegboard. Sets of plastic letters and numbers of various sizes can also be bought. These clip into the holes of the pegboard, and serve both to draw attention to the display, and to give extra information needed concerning its contents.

One of the purposes of displaying a selection of non-fiction is to draw the borrowers' attention to books allied to his own subject, which are placed in different sections of the library's classification system. Plastic pegboard numbers give the opportunity to indicate the classification numbers of displayed books and thus broaden the borrower's knowledge of the classification scheme. If pegboard is not available coloured sugar paper can be used for backcloth display, and this gives the opportunity to introduce eye-catching contrast by using, for instance, black sugar paper for the mounting of light pictures or photographs. Coloured and contrasting string, tapes and ribbons serve the same purpose. They are fastened to the backcloth or pegboard and sloped downwards to connect the books with their related cuttings, captions, photographs and classification numbers, thus forming effective attention-directing devices.

The lettering used for display work and posters should always be simple, so as to be eye-catching from a distance. Proficiency in the use of one or more of the many types of instant lettering kits now available can save both time and the unnecessary effort involved in producing free-hand lettering. There are also stencilling kits which involve blocking in spaces with chunky paint brushes, and others with letters that have to be traced around. Even easier to handle are the pre-cut letters with an adhesive backing which can be used over and over again. For smaller lettering purposes there are sheets of pre-printed letters which are processed by either being peeled off or by being rubbed on to the paper or cardboard. Though not as yet universally used, a jumbo or macro typewriter produces giant sized letters for effective display work in the shortest possible time of all.

Finally displays should never be allowed to look 'frayed' round the edges, or otherwise neglected. They require to be changed frequently and regularly if their purpose is to be achieved. Before the next change of display takes place, however, it is important to have a sketch of the display made, and also a list of all the books used to illustrate the theme. These can be stored in a folder along with any other display material thought worth keeping to form the basis of any similar display in the future.

A library's appearance can make or mar a borrower's pleasure in his surroundings. The good housekeeping aspect of librarianship is one in which the library assistant has a vital role to play.

Assignments
1 Describe the steps you would take if asked to arrange a library display on 'house maintenance'.
2 Explain the reasons why books are sometimes arranged out of sequence in a library, and suggest ways in which readers' attention may be drawn to such books.
3 Consider the stock of your own library to find out what is done in the way of minor repairs to prolong the life of books and *two* other types of printed materials.

4 Books are often missing from their correct place on the shelves. Explain how the duties undertaken by a library assistant can ensure their speedy return.

Chapter 8

LENDING PROCEDURES

Reader registration
Many libraries keep a record of those persons who are entitled
to use the library, so that they can be easily identified. Many
educational and special libraries dispense with the register of
readers, usually because membership details are available
elsewhere within the organization.

In public libraries a readers' register is essential, and is usually
compiled by filing membership application cards. Potential
readers are asked to complete a form giving personal details, and
which usually includes an undertaking to comply with the rules
of that library. The readers' eligibility for membership is usually
established by referring to the electoral roll for that area. The
reader receives his membership card or tickets, and the
application card is then filed in a register of borrowers.

Some public libraries permit adult readers to become members
without guarantors. Most libraries permit residents to register on
their own signature, but non-residents may need suitably
qualified persons to countersign their application forms. Some
libraries may use different forms for the two categories of user,
or in some cases, different coloured forms. These forms are then
checked against the defaulters' file, which is a list of readers who
have failed to return books or refused to pay fines. The application
forms are usually valid for three years at a time, and readers may
be asked to renew their membership when their tickets expire.
The use of coloured tickets can make expiry self-evident. Some
libraries send membership cards or tickets to their new readers
by post, thus ensuring that the postal information on the
application card is correct.

People who work or attend colleges or schools in the area are
often permitted to become members at the nearest public library,

regardless of where they live. Many library authorities allow readers to use tickets from other authorities at their libraries and this inter-availability of membership is very useful especially when on holiday, although there may be difficulties arising from different issue systems which may be in use.

Changes of address or surname, e.g. on marriage, should be recorded promptly in the readers' register and also on the readers' tickets. From time to time readers may report lost tickets, and each library will have suitable procedures for dealing with this problem. Some may charge a fee for replacement tickets, depending on the method of issue used at that library, for in some cases a missing ticket will correspond to a missing book which may never be recovered.

Byelaws and regulations

A public library authority may make byelaws to prevent damage to library premises and their contents, and to ensure the proper behaviour of library users. Library byelaws must be submitted to the Department of Education and Science for confirmation, then printed and prominently displayed. Copies must also be available to the general public on request. People who offend against byelaws can be prosecuted in Magistrates' courts, and may be fined. A set of model byelaws has been published by the Library Association.

Library regulations do not require confirmation by the DES, and cannot be enforced at law. They usually define how library procedures, such as the loan of materials, are to be carried out so that readers can be treated fairly and consistently. Academic libraries have similar rules to regulate the use of their facilities and services, and they may withdraw membership from those people who persistently refuse to follow them.

Issue systems

Each library will use a system for recording the books or other items that it lends to its readers. There have been many modern developments to record issues in the last 30 years, mainly due to the high cost of staffing, increased usage, and in search of better all round efficiency.

A good system should enable the library staff to discover which reader has borrowed which books. It should show when the books are due for return and which are overdue. Some systems can control the number of books issued, and particularly the number which each reader has borrowed. The better systems will permit issues to be renewed without returning the book in person, and should allow readers to reserve books which are not immediately available. All these transactions should be done speedily, or else some facility introduced which permits work to be completed later without the reader being kept waiting. Lastly, statistics of various types will be very helpful, and should be capable of collection from the issue system without too much trouble.

Browne

The Browne system of issuing books was used in most public libraries for many years, and is still very common, especially in branch libraries where the volume of issues does not warrant a more sophisticated system.

Each lending book has a bookcard which is kept in a pocket inside each book. The bookcard identifies each book by recording, usually, the accession number, classification number, author and short title. Each reader has tickets issued to him which indicate his name and address. This reader's ticket holds the bookcard, which is taken from the pocket in the book, and this forms the record of the issue. Each book is stamped with the date for return and the issue is filed in trays under the date due for return, and within that date probably by accession number.

When the reader returns the book, the date due for return stamped on the date label locates the correct date among the issue trays and the accession number printed on the date label should find the correct position within that date. The bookcard is then returned to the book, which is now ready for shelving, and the reader recovers his ticket. If problems occur the reader is detained until his ticket is found, or until a temporary ticket is prepared. Overdue books are self-evident since the trays are in date order, and reservations are made by searching the issue date by date, and then marking the appropriate card in an obvious way.

It is slower to return books than it is to issue them, and over a certain capacity saturation point can be reached where assistants cannot work any faster, and queues begin to form at the library entrance. Unfortunately, more assistants do not greatly increase the speed, since they tend to slow each other down, as they each jostle for access to the same trays. The Browne system is simply operated and easily understood by library staff and readers alike. It is familiar and has been the most popular long-standing system in use in Britain. Now, increasing demands have shown that it lacks the capability of dealing with busy periods and consistently large issues. In most central libraries it has been superseded by mechanized systems.

Computer charging

In recent years, more and more libraries have introduced computerized issue systems to offer improved services both for readers and staff. Computers can deal speedily and accurately with great amounts of data, and can also give instant reserve and overdue facilities which other systems may find difficult to provide.

A typical computer charging system identifies books and readers by bar-coded labels, mounted on each book and on readers' cards. A sensing device, usually a light pen, reads the labels and automatically records the information. The date due for return is stamped on the date label, the borrower's card is returned and the transaction is complete. When the book is returned, only the book label needs to be read by the light pen.

Other systems provide book labels which are fixed to the inside back cover of books. A reading head which can penetrate book covers can be used so that books need not be opened, but are merely slid along the counter over the reading device.

Most systems are supplied with trapping stores which contain the numbers of reserved books, and which check each transaction and signal when a reserved book is returned. Book numbers are added to the store or deleted by a numerical keyboard. Trapping stores can also be used to identify specific borrowers when necessary. Renewals are quite simple, requiring book and borrower numbers to be recorded on a keyboard. The trapping store will detect reserves at the renewal stage. Overdue notices are produced by the computer when required. Of course, computers can produce an endless variety of statistics based on the data recorded at the issue counter, and a great amount of useful information can be obtained very easily.

Triplicate record

Some eduational and special libraries require borrowers to complete an issue form each time a book is borrowed. Suitable forms are usually divided into three parts and information is tranferred by carbons. When the form is completed, it can be separated. The top copy is usually filed by book number within the date due back, and the bottom copy is usually filed under the reader's surname. The third copy can be used as an overdue reminder if required. When the book is returned the matching slips are found and destroyed. This system is slow and laborious for the reader. It saves the writing of bookcards and tickets, and returned books can be traced in the issue later, when the reader has left. It is most suitable for small libraries where staff time is short.

Detection devices

Many modern libraries include detection devices at their issue desks to act as a deterrent to would-be thieves. Some systems work on a magnetic principle. Each book is fitted with a trigger, which is a small metal strip usually attached inside the spine of the book. Triggers are sensitized with automatic equipment, as books are returned. Books which are being taken from the library pass through two detection pillars at either side of the exit. Unless the books have been desensitized, when they were properly issued, they will activate an audio or visual alarm system, which can be fitted to a locking turnstile or door. Equipment at the entrance point effectively neutralizes most common metal objects to avoid false alarms.

Other systems use simple pressure sensitive labels which incorporate a simple printed circuit and can be quickly fixed on to or inside books and other items to be protected. A very low frequency radio signal activates the label triggers. The manufacturers maintain that their equipment is safe and reliable, and that no commonly carried objects will give false alarms, so that staff may confidently challenge readers whenever necessary. These systems which operate electronically can be effectively incorporated with computer issue systems. When properly installed and operated, all systems are highly successful in reducing the theft of library materials.

81

Public Lending Right

The Public Lending Right Act was passed in 1979 to enable authors to receive payment to compensate for the loss of income incurred as a result of their books being freely available to readers through public libraries in Great Britain.

All the money needed to finance Public Lending Right is provided by the Government in a Central Fund. Authors wishing to draw from this fund must register and claims are assessed according to the number of times their books have been borrowed based on loan records from sample libraries.

Book reservations

When a reader reserves a book, the catalogue should be checked to see whether the library holds a copy of the title requested. If so, the shelves should be checked to locate the reserved book, and if the book is on loan, then the appropriate procedure for tracing and stopping the book in the issue should be followed, depending on the issue system in use. When the book is returned it is held on a reservations shelf and the reader is notified by post that the reserved book is ready for collection.

If the library does not hold a copy, the details should be carefully checked and the union catalogue consulted to make sure that the title is not held elsewhere within the library system, before passing the request to the Inter-Library Loans Section, where the title will be identified by its ISBN or BNB number and a request sent to the local Regional Library Bureau.

Regional library systems

Each library cannot be self-sufficient for all titles or categories of material, and the Regional Library Interlending System was set up, from 1930 onwards, so that participating libraries could draw upon the resources of member libraries when necessary. The country is divided into nine regions including Scotland and Wales (see Figure 4). Within each region, all public libraries and several academic and special libraries agree to lend material to each other on request. The interlending scheme is administered by a Bureau in each region whose function is to maintain a union catalogue of the stocks of all member libraries in the Region, and to monitor and allocate requests so that the interlending is spread as evenly as possible among the participating libraries. Requests to the

National Library
of Scotland

Northern Regional Library System
Cleveland
Cumbria
Durham
Northumberland
Tyne & Wear

Yorkshire & Humberside
Joint Library Services
Humberside
North Yorkshire
South Yorkshire
West Yorkshire

North Western
Regional
Library System
Cheshire
Greater Manchester
Lancashire
Merseyside

East Midlands
Regional Library
System
Cambridgeshire
Derbyshire
Leicestershire
Lincolnshire
Norfolk
Northamptonshire
Nottinghamshire
Suffolk

BLDSC

West Midlands Regional
Library Bureau
Hereford & Worcester
Salop
Staffordshire
Warwickshire
West Midlands

Wales Regional
Library Scheme
Clwyd
Dyfed
Glamorgan
Gwent
Gwynedd
Powys

South West
Regional Library System
Avon
Cornwall
Devon
Dorset
Gloucestershire
Hampshire
Isle of Wight
Oxfordshire
Somerset
Wiltshire

Edinburgh

Newcastle

Boston
Spa

Wakefield

Manchester

Aberystwyth

Leicester

Birmingham

Bristol

London

LASER
Bedfordshire
Berkshire
Buckinghamshire
East Sussex
Essex

Greater London
Hertfordshire
Kent
Surrey
West Sussex

Figure 4: British regional library systems

Bureau are made on printed forms which are checked against the union catalogue to find locations and are then circulated on a rota to libraries who hold the requested books, until the request is satisfied, or until the list of locations is exhausted. On receiving such a request, a library will check its shelves and issue, supply the requested item by post to the borrowing library, or pass the request to the next library on the list. Requests for urgent material can be made to the Bureau by telephone or telex, and an immediate location will be given for the lending library to be approached directly. Some Regions have produced ISBN location indexes or even full union catalogues or microfiche, so that member libraries can obtain immediate locations for reserved material. If the Bureau is unable to give locations, then the requests will be passed on to the British Library Document Supply Centre, or libraries may apply there in the first place for material which is known to be in short supply in the Region, such as foreign material and specialized scientific and technical publications particularly in serial or report format.

British Library Document Supply Centre
The British Library Document Supply Centre, formerly the British Library Lending Division, is situated in Yorkshire and was established in 1973 by the amalgamation of the National Central Library and the National Lending Library for Science and Technology. Its purpose is to supply libraries speedily with loans and photocopies of material from stock which are not easily available elsewhere. A large collection of material has been built up to satisfy this demand, and items not included may be located from other specialist libraries acting as back up suppliers.

BLDSC is currently building collections of material known as likely to be needed for inter-library lending, excluding children's books, fiction and ephemera. Requests are made on pre-paid application forms purchased by the borrowing libraries. Part of the purchase price of the application form is to offset delivery and packing charges, and failed requests are refunded. Users may make urgent requests by telephone or telex, but a request form identification number must also be quoted.

BLDSC has now produced a catalogue of its current book acquisitions on microfiche, and this is now also available online through BLAISE-LINE, so that required items can be checked for availability and loan requests can be recorded instantly. This additional service eliminates unnecessary delays and avoids the uncertainties of speculative applications. It is quick, cheap and easy to use.

Loans and photocopies are usually provided within a few days, and are lent for a minimum period of three weeks. Eighty-four per cent of requests are supplied from stock and a further nine per cent from back up libraries. Average daily requests number 11,000, reaching over three million each year. BLDSC will not accept subject enquiries, and the borrowing library is responsible for any bibliographical searching which may be required on behalf of readers. Most requests are supplied by post, although some regions have direct van service links with BLDSC, ensuring rapid, reliable handling of requests.

Local cooperation

Several cooperative schemes have been established on a local basis in order to provide literature and information quickly and effectively, within well-defined geographical areas. Usually, these local cooperative schemes have developed in response to demands for specialized material from local industry and commerce. A large city reference library or commercial and technical department will frequently form the headquarters, and a catalogue with locations from neighbouring libraries will give locations for requests. Special collections of directories, abstracts and indexes, translation services and sources of periodical holdings will also be provided.

A pioneering scheme was the Sheffield Interchange Organization (SINTO), started in 1933 with specialized subject collections on the steel industry, based on Sheffield City Libraries Commercial and Technical Department. Several other major cities have developed similar schemes, and one other example worthy of note is the Hertfordshire Technical Information Service (HERTIS) based on successful cooperation between the county library service and further education colleges in the area, the librarian of Hatfield Polytechnic being also the County Technical Librarian. This scheme goes some way towards compensating for the lack of a large central reference library in a county area.

Further local cooperative initiatives may include agreements on the cooperative purchase and storage of specialist material, staff training, local transport or computer applications.

Assignments
1 What clerical routines are involved in registering new readers in a library, and how would you introduce a new reader to the services available in your library? (CGLI 1987)
2 With reference to *either* the Browne charging system *or* a computer charging system, describe briefly the processes involved in
   a renewing lost tickets
   b locating reserved books
   c recording change of address
   d collecting fines on overdue books.
   (CGLI 1986)
3 Which library routines might be improved by the introduction of new technology? What are the possible disadvantages of computer-based systems? (CGLI 1987)
4 Some libraries do not restrict borrowers to a specific number of books on loan at a time. What advantages and disadvantages will result from such a policy? (CGLI 1978)
5 How may theft of library materials and unauthorized borrowing be kept to a minimum? (CGLI 1978)
6 Explain how the inter-library loan system operates in the United Kingdom, and describe some of the routines carried out by an assistant in your library who wants to obtain a publication from elsewhere. (CGLI 1986)

Chapter 9

ENQUIRIES AND REFERENCE MATERIAL

Library assistants may frequently deal with simple reference enquiries. Often they are the first point of enquiry for readers and can gather useful experience of dealing with the public and using reference material in this way. It is important to be familiar with the commoner reference books to be found in most libraries. This familiarity can only be acquired by using and handling such material as often as possible. The contents, coverage, frequency and arrangement should be carefully noted, and any new reference books should be examined as they arrive.

When a reader first makes his enquiry, he should be questioned to discover what is really required. This is often difficult since readers are often unsure themselves, and misleading approaches can waste time for both the assistant and the reader. The reader should be asked if the information is urgent, or if any deadline applies. The assistant must not keep the enquirer waiting unduly, and should take the name, address and telephone number almost at once if the enquirer has telephoned, or if a quick preliminary search indicates that more time will be needed.

The information search should be organized and systematic. The assistant should work from the general to the particular. An encyclopaedia article may provide an initial survey of the subject. The library shelves should be checked for a standard text or a general book containing the subject. If there is no suitable book on the shelves, the library catalogue should be checked for pamphlets, oversize books and added entries. Different approaches via the classification system may be tried, not forgetting special categories of material where applicable, e.g. government publications, trade literature, statistics. Abstracts and periodical indexes should be checked, and, if appropriate, newspaper indexes and latest issues. Any appropriate computer databases or viewdata sources, such as Prestel, should also be checked if necessary. The library's own index of difficult queries and information file may also prove useful. Colleagues should be consulted to ensure that all possibilities have been tried. Now that the library's own stock has been covered, it is useful to give the reader an interim report. Sometimes, the material already discovered will be sufficient, and sometimes the enquiry may have been satisfied elsewhere in the meantime.

If the enquiry is to proceed beyond the library's own resources, bibliographies and catalogues of other libraries must be consulted. References that have now been gathered, and articles in periodicals not held can now be obtained through the Regional Library Bureau or the British Library Document Supply Centre. Personal contacts may also be tried. Individual experts, societies, government departments, industrial sources may each be approached if applicable, and duly recorded for the next time.

Every book and entry should be recorded to avoid repetition, especially when passing the enquiry on to others. Experienced assistants often get speedy results by different procedures and approaches, but no reader should be left with a negative answer to his enquiry. However, only published authoritative information is required. Personal opinions are only valid where the source is professionally competent, and of course the assistant must never tender such an opinion.

Bibliographies

Bibliographies are lists of books and are compiled in many different forms. They are important for book selection and for finding out about individual books. Authors and titles can be traced and sometimes subject enquiries can be followed. Most libraries will have copies of the basic general bibliographies for British books. Usually they are kept at the readers' adviser's desk, but assistants will need to use them frequently for checking reserves, order cards and simple enquiries.

Books in English records those books listed in the combined Library of Congress and British National Bibliography computer database, and is the largest current bibliography of English language books published throughout the world. It is an author and title list with full catalogue entries, and Library of Congress and Dewey classification numbers. Each issue is fully cumulated, and is produced every two months on ultra microfiche, reduced 150 times, with up to 3,000 pages on each fiche, requiring special microreading machines for its use. Over 100,000 books are listed each year, and there is now a 1971–1980 cumulation, combining the ten annual listings into a single sequence. It is as near as possible to being a comprehensive bibliography of English language books.

The *British national bibliography* started in 1950 and is issued weekly with interim and annual cumulations. The preface describes it as 'a list of new British books received by the Copyright Receipt Office of the British Library, arranged according to the 19th edition of the Dewey Decimal Classification and catalogued according to the provisions of the second edition of the Anglo-American Cataloguing Rules'. It is a comprehensive list of new and forthcoming British books, excluding cheap novelettes, music, maps, minor government publications, and periodicals other than the first issue. It sets out to describe each work in detail, supplying a full catalogue entry, and giving the subject matter of each as accurately as possible. Some entries are prepared from advance information supplied by the publisher, and not from the books themselves. These entries are indicated by the abbreviation CIP (Cataloguing in Publication). Each weekly list contains an index of authors, titles and series. Two separate indexes of authors and titles and of subjects covering all items in the weekly lists for each month appear in the last weekly list of the month. There are January to April, and May to August cumulations, followed by an annual volume and five-yearly cumulations, although no cumulated volumes have appeared since 1973. There is now available a 1950–1984 cumulation on microfiche, which covers 35 years of British publishing in a single author-title bibliography, and a 1981–5 complete cumulation with subject classified entries in addition. It is the authoritative current British bibliography produced by the British Library Bibliographic Services Division. Records from the British National Bibliography are included in the UK MARC (Machine Readable Cataloguing) files, and can be retrieved via BLAISE and held in computer systems by local libraries, thus avoiding duplication of cataloguing effort.

Whitaker's books in print (formerly known as *British books in print*) is an essential guide to British books available and on sale in bookshops each year. It contains a list of British publishers, followed by the main section comprising a combined author and title list of books currently available, whether newly published or not. In printed form *WBIP* contains over 7,000 pages in four volumes, listing over 400,000 titles in print in the UK. Since 1978 *WBIP* has been issued in a microfiche edition, updated and cumulated each month. This gives much greater currency with regard to availability and prices. Each month there are 4,500 new titles added, 3,000 out of print titles removed and 50,000 price alterations. In January and July each year special fiches of Forthcoming Books are included. Also now available is *Books 1976 – 87 now OP* on microfiche listing 180,000 titles published between 1976 and 1987 which are no longer available. Another additional service is *ISBN listing* issued twice per year, which gives 900,000 titles in ISBN sequence with out of print books clearly indicated.

Soon *WBIP* will be available on CD-ROMs which are compact discs capable of storing vast amounts of digital data that can be read by laser in a CD-ROM reader linked to a microcomputer. It will be known as *Whitaker's bookbank CD-ROM service*. Two important advantages of CD-ROM as a medium are the increase in the number of access or search factors to the book information that can be tried, and the ability to copy selected data from CD-ROM electronically into library computers for use in acquisitions or cataloguing systems. *WBIP* is also available as a computer database which can be accessed online via the British Library's BLAISE-LINE, and also via DIALOG.

Most public libraries subscribe to *The bookseller*, a weekly trade magazine for the British book industry, which contains a list entitled 'Publications of the week', which is a weekly update of newly published titles. Here, new books including reprints, re-issues and new editions are listed alphabetically under author, title and subject keyword where this is part of the title. The entry includes price, and an abbreviation indicating the broad classification of the book. Two large Spring and Autumn preview issues are produced, providing useful advance information about forthcoming books. *Whitaker's books of the month and books to come* is a monthly update of newly published titles, which includes books due for publication in the next two months, and *Whitaker's cumulative book list* is an annual update of all titles published.

The *British catalogue of audio-visual materials* is based on the holdings of the Inner London Education Authority's Central Library Resources Service. It is published by the British Library Bibliographic Services Division and its arrangement is similar to that of the *British national bibliography*, with a Dewey classified sequence, followed by an alphabetical index of titles, series and names, and an alphabetical subject index. It covers all audio-visual materials except video recordings, 16mm films and musical sound recordings, many of which are listed elsewhere. A second Supplement was issued in 1983.

Government publications
British government publications are prepared and issued by Her Majesty's Stationery Office. With an estimated 40,000 titles in print, they form a large and important publishing undertaking, whose subject coverage is wide and varied, except for subjects such as philosophy, religion or pure literature. Tracing official publications can be difficult since only a selection is included in *BNB*, but there are several lists available issued by HMSO to enable customers to identify all their publications quickly and reliably.

The *Daily list of government publications* is issued each day except public holidays and weekends and can be posted to libraries daily or in weekly batches. Its five sections cover Parliamentary papers, non-Parliamentary papers arranged by Ministries and departments, reprints and items sold but not published by HMSO, publications of international organizations like the United Nations, and statutory instruments which are mainly legal or administrative regulations. The *Daily list* is invaluable to those who need to know quickly what is being published by the Government. The *Monthly catalogue of government publications* contains three sections covering Parliamentary papers, a classified list of mainly non-Parliamentary papers, and periodicals. It excludes statutory instruments, and has an index of subjects, brief titles and personal names. The *Annual catalogue of government publications* omits statutory instruments and specialized material such as Admiralty charts, Ordnance Survey maps, and patents. An annual catalogue of *International organizations' publications* is issued separately. All HMSO publications in print and available are listed in the quarterly *HMSO in print on microfiche*. Items are included under several headings such as title, author, department and chairman. It is a valuable reference source to the great range of HMSO publications. Current HMSO titles are listed on Prestel on the day they are announced and for a further week, and can be ordered via Prestel. There are also plans for online access to HMSO's own bibliographic services database.

Other useful guides to British government publications are the *Sectional lists* which are issued free. They cover most government departments listing the current non-Parliamentary publications of each department, with a selection of Parliamentary papers. The series which has been recently updated comprises nearly 30 lists which are regularly revised.

The most famous British government publication is *Hansard's Parliamentary debates* which is a verbatim account of all Parliamentary business. It is published daily while Parliament is sitting, and is cumulated into bound volumes with detailed indexes of subjects and speakers. There is also a weekly *Hansard*. Another well-known publication is *Britain: an official handbook* issued annually by HMSO, which gives outline statistics and basic information on many aspects of British life.

Periodicals

Periodicals provide up-to-date information and news in advance of books, not only in articles, but in reviews and announcements. More advanced journals are the normal channels for news of research, and many contain the most up-to-date information. Back files of periodicals are often the only source of information on minor topics, and can provide brief summaries for hurried readers. They are often an important source for illustrations which cannot be found elsewhere, and they are the principal source for contemporary opinion of historical events. They are also frequently the only source for information on people and topics that were once well-known but are now forgotten.

Guides help to identify and describe periodicals and newspapers. *Current British journals*, which was first published in 1970, is now in its fourth edition. It is produced by the United Kingdom Serials Group, an autonomous body made up of librarians, booksellers, serials agents, and publishers and represents all who are interested in every aspect of serial provision. Entries for about 7,000 British journals are arranged in UDC classified order. Basic information is provided for each title, including the availability of indexes and the existence of microform editions. There are plans to revise and update the work more frequently.

An important annual British trade guide is *Willings press guide*. It is an alphabetical list of newspapers and periodicals in the United Kingdom, including the year of establishment, the publisher's name and address, price, frequency and day of publication. There is a section classified by subject which is extremely useful. Overseas publications are arranged by country. There is also a Newspaper Index, a list of UK publications and their titles, and services and supplies.

Benn's media directory, formerly entitled the *Newspaper press directory*, gives an up-to-date and impartial view of the media scene. Its main sections cover a County/Regional Index to newspapers, classified indexes to periodicals, directories, agencies and services, and a Master A – Z index to all listed UK publishers. There is an important Broadcasting Section which covers the BBC, IBA, commercial radio and television, both cable and satellite, and electronic publishing.

The British Library Document Supply Centre produces an annual list of *Current serials received*, which is a title list of over 50,000 journals on all subjects. It includes Cyrillic serials and cover to cover translations of Cyrillic serials.

Indexes to periodicals are essential for tracing references and subject enquiries for files which are held elsewhere. The *British humanities index* began in 1962, succeeding the *Library Association subject index to periodicals* which was first published in 1915. It is issued quarterly, with an annual cumulation. Periodical articles are indexed alphabetically by subjects, and there is an author index. About 400 British journals are indexed and coverage includes politics, economics, history, literature, philosophy, religion and law. A sister publication is the *Current technology index*, which began in 1962 and is published by the Library Association. *CTI* is issued monthly, with a cumulated annual volume. Subject headings are arranged alphabetically, and there is an author index. Subjects cover all fields of engineering and chemical technology, including the manufactures based upon them. It omits agriculture and medicine. In 1981, *Current technology index* extended its coverage to include several additional journals. In 1987, the Library Association began publication of *Applied social sciences index and abstracts (ASSIA)* which provides comprehensive coverage of English language material – over 500 journals indexed from over 20 countries. Its subject coverage is wide ranging and it should prove invaluable for those working in applied social sciences, as well as being extremely useful for those in related fields. *ASSIA* is issued six times per year and there is an annual cumulation.

Newspapers provide the most up-to-date information and are often the starting point for readers' enquiries. A national daily and the local newspaper should be taken and held by most libraries. Back files are useful if they are indexed. Indexes to *The Times* have been commercially available for many years, and now indexes to *The Guardian* and *The Financial Times* can be obtained.

Keesings record of world events is a digest or summary of news from Britain and overseas, providing impartial and authoritative information on international current affairs. To ensure that the information is as up-to-date as possible sections are posted to subscribers monthly for insertion in loose-leaf binders, and the arrangement is therefore chronological. There are interim indexes of subjects and names, which are also revised at the end of each year.

Dictionaries and encyclopaedias

Dictionaries give the meaning, spelling and pronunciation of words and are arranged alphabetically. The *New English dictionary* commonly called the 'Oxford', is by far the most comprehensive and detailed English dictionary. It is concerned not only with current usage, but also with the history and development of words, and because of its bulk it is not easy to use. It is published in 12 volumes with supplements, and there is a cheaper compact edition which can be read with the help of a magnifying glass. The *Shorter Oxford dictionary* (2 vols.) contains about two-thirds of the words in the main work, and the *Concise Oxford dictionary* is a smaller one-volume edition.

There are many comprehensive one-volume dictionaries, and a typical example is *Chamber's twentieth century dictionary*. This contains entries for 250,000 words and aims to include 'all words in general use in literary and conversational English, plus specialist vocabularies from science, medicine and technology'.

94

The entries include pronunciation, parts of speech, meanings, derivations (phrases and hyphenated forms) and brief etymology. Appendices include lists of foreign phrases, common abbreviations, musical and mathematical symbols and English Christian names. No dictionary is more frequently revised and updated, thus ensuring that it can be relied upon to reflect the language of today.

Roget's thesaurus of English words and phrases gives antonyms and synonyms arranged according to their meanings, or the ideas that they express. For the most effective use, the index is essential. A *concordance* lists all the important words in a particular book and shows where they may be found in that book. *Cruden's complete concordance* to the Old and New Testament, first compiled in 1737, contains over 250,000 entries including all personal and place names in the Bible.

Encyclopaedias give short accounts of surveys of various subjects, and provide basic factual information. *Hutchinson's new twentieth century encyclopaedia* is a good example of a one-volume encyclopaedia with many short articles and *Pear's cyclopaedia* is an authoritative and compact family reference book published annually. *Everyman's encyclopaedia* is in ten volumes with about 50,000 articles giving 'rapid information on all subjects encountered in the general course of reading or everyday affairs'. There are short, up-to-date articles on scientific subjects, with many illustrations, but there is no general index.

The *Encyclopaedia Britannica* is an outstanding general encyclopaedia now in its 15th edition. The encyclopaedia is a little confusing to use at first. It is therefore important for assistants to become familiar with its use and arrangement so that readers can be guided when necessary. The first 12 volumes form the Micropaedia or ready-reference facility supplying short entries which may lead to more detailed articles in other volumes of the encyclopaedia. The Macropaedia in 17 further volumes is the main body of the encyclopaedia giving extended treatment of human knowledge in depth. There is also a one-volume Propaedia or outline of knowledge which acts as a study guide to the encyclopaedia. New to this edition is a comprehensive two-volume index providing over 170,000 entries that guide readers with over 400,000 references to information contained in the main encyclopaedia.

A typical encyclopaedia of a special subject is the *McGraw-Hill encyclopaedia of science and technology* issued in 20 revised volumes. It is intended 'to provide the widest possible range of articles that will be understandable and useful to any person of modest technical training who wants to obtain information outside his particular field of specialization'. It is American in origin and covers the whole field of science and technology, except history and philosophy, and it is simple to understand and use, with up-to-the-minute coverage of all major new developments in science.

Reference books

A reference book is one which is specially compiled and arranged to supply information and facts, rather than to be read continuously. There are many varied types of reference books, and a selection of those which might be found in most libraries is described here.

The *Guinness book of records* is one of the most successful reference books ever devised, and it is most popular with children. Its contents are arranged into 12 parts, and there is a strong emphasis on sporting information. There are many illustrations and a good index.

Whitaker's almanack is an annual publication giving general information. It is an encyclopaedia, a directory and an annual survey rolled into one. Particularly important is the review of political, scientific, sporting and cultural events of the preceding year. No single book contains as much information although much of it is often very brief, and it is usually the first checkpoint for most general reference enquiries. The useful general index is at the front.

The *Statesman's yearbook* is an annual reference book on the countries of the world containing an outline of political, economic, cultural and statistical information, including industries, natural resources, a bibliography and diplomatic representatives. It is arranged in two parts: International Organizations, including the United Nations and its agencies, and Countries of the World arranged alphabetically.

The *Citizens advice notes service* was originally produced for the use of staffs in Citizens Advice Bureaux. In classified form, it provides information on current legislation and administrative regulations affecting daily life and needs. It gives a concise statement of the current legal position on areas such as housing, education, employment and social services, and it is kept up-to-date by regular supplements. The arrangement is in sections which are numbered within each section, making the detailed index at the front essential for proper use.

The standard reference book for local government in the United Kingdom is the *Municipal year book*. It reviews the previous year's work, then lists all local authorities giving details such as population, area, finance, members, chief officers, in addition to statistical tables on local government activities such as housing and education. The index is at the front, and there are sections on public services, government departments, and development corporations.

Kelly's business directory is an annual reference work recognized throughout the world as the leading buyer's guide to British industry and commerce. It includes the name, address, telephone number and trade description of over 84,000 organizations engaged in industry and commerce in the UK. It includes a large classified section with over 10,000 trade and professional headings. There is a useful section on Brand and Trade Names and one on International Exporters. *Kompass UK* lists the suppliers of 35,000 products and services by the main industrial groups, and gives company information arranged geographically.

Telephone directories should not be ignored. They are useful sources of information on addresses and trade enquiries. They also supply details such as correct postal addresses and emergency services. Classified directories and *Yellow pages* include entries under trades, manufacturers and professions. There is no other reference book which is more taken for granted.

Kempe's engineer's year book is produced annually and supplies information for all engineering enquiries. There are 90 sections, over 3,000 pages and chapters on patents, design, trade marks, legal notes for engineers, and useful bibliographies.

The *Dictionary of national biography* is the most important retrospective reference work of English biography. It is issued in 22 volumes, with supplements up to 1970. It contains lengthy, signed articles with good bibliographies. The *Concise DNB* has brief versions of all the entries and serves as both a summary and an index to the main work. *Who's who* is the leading British biographical dictionary of living people, with approximately

30,000 entries. People are included for their personal achievement or prominence and interest to the public at large. Entries are compiled from information supplied by the subjects themselves and include full name, description, date of birth, children, education, activities, publications, recreations, dates and telephone numbers. There is additional information on the Royal Family, the New Year's Honours List, a list of abbreviations, and an obituary.

Atlases and gazetteers
Atlases are bound volumes of maps, charts and tables, which are essential for the study of geography and may also be useful for information on current affairs. *The times atlas of the world* is a comprehensive and reliable reference work with over 130 maps, and with an index on world resources.

Gazetteers give the location of places, together with appropriate economic or historical information. *Bartholomew's gazetteer of Britain* has 40,000 entries and gives National Grid references. Being fairly recent in publication, it includes the new place names created during local government reorganization in Great Britain.

Motoring handbooks contain lists of towns and provide details of hotels, garages, population and early closing days. They contain detailed road maps and town plans, and supply full information of the services offered to members. The *Royal Automobile Club handbook* is issued annually and is generally available, the *Automobile Association handbook* is for members only.

AA town plans is an atlas covering 64 major towns and cities in Britain with many clear plans covering town centres, and suburban main routes. They show one-way systems, parking facilities, principal shopping areas and list public buildings and places of interest.

Information file
Every library should have its own information file which should contain, among other details, the addresses and telephone numbers of local council offices, government departments, local chambers of commerce, associations, societies, churches, schools, travel offices, police stations and emergency services. In fact, all or any local information thought to be useful, which is not readily available elsewhere should be immediately accessible here.

Not all the reference books mentioned here will be available in every library, but most should be. The efficient library assistant will know that they exist and will know how to locate and use them when necessary.

Assignments
1 Describe the contents of the annual volume of the *British national bibliography*. (CGLI 1976)
2 List and describe the main official guides to the publications issued by Her Majesty's Stationery Office. (CGLI 1978)
3 What is the *British humanities index*? State:
   a how it is published
   b its coverage
   c its use by librarians.
   (CGLI 1971)
4 Describe three different ways of keeping reference books up to date. (CGLI 1978)
5 Select *five* of the following topics and name one directory or year book giving information about each. Do not quote the same title more than once.
   A person
   A place
   A company
   A newspaper
   A library
   A particular industry
   A telegraphic address
   A telex.
   (CGLI 1972)

Chapter 10

OFFICE PRACTICE

All clerical workers need to be both tidy and methodical in their work. There are special reasons why it is even more important for library assistants to practise neatness and orderliness in carrying out their clerical duties.

Unlike most offices, libraries cannot allocate a desk or individual working space to each member of staff. Library assistants have to be prepared to carry out duties in many areas of the library, according to the nature of the task in hand. Assistants work intermittently on their clerical duties, often being called, for example, to address overdue postcards, whilst at the same time manning the issue desk and attending to readers. Most libraries have a longer working day than the average office, and to cover the long opening hours, including the evening sessions, it is necessary to organize staff timetables on a variable shift system. This can result in work being started by one assistant and completed by another. Since many clerical duties are carried out in the public sector of the library, this means that work is frequently interrupted to attend to readers. For all these reasons careful thought has to be given to setting up clerical working space, to procedures for when work is interrupted, or has to be left for someone else to complete, and also to leaving the working area in good order when the task is finished.

Many routine jobs include the copying of information – from membership forms, readers' tickets, and issue cards for example. These should be placed at the left of the working space, and once the information has been recorded or transferred, the card or ticket should be reversed and placed face downwards on the right hand side. As each item is dealt with, it should be similarly added to the right hand pile, thus maintaining the same order throughout the operation. If staff are called away, another assistant will be clearly able to continue the task at a later time. If work has to be left for longer than the odd minute or so, care should be taken to secure the two piles of documents to prevent confusion. When handling catalogue cards it is useful to insert a card at right angles, so that it protrudes, clearly indicating how far the work has progressed. A pencilled note on the card will act as an added precaution in case the card should be removed or reinserted wrongly.

Once a task is completed, the working space must be cleared of all work. All cards and tickets must be reinserted in sequence in their tray, and any misused stationery should be destroyed. Any items of equipment that have been used should be carefully returned to their places, so that the next user does not waste time searching for them. Above all, particularly for on-coming part-time staff, precise messages and clear instructions should be left to ensure continuity and to prevent confusion.

Post

Most libraries will have a postal delivery each day, and some will have such large amounts of post to deal with that it becomes important to establish regular procedures for handling and sorting post in a consistent and orderly manner. The post must be attended to early in the day, because many of the items delivered may affect the work of the library and need to be distributed internally as soon as possible.

Envelopes marked 'confidential', 'personal', or 'private' should not be opened, but should be delivered intact. Other items should be opened carefully and their contents unfolded. Any enclosures should be neatly attached, any cheques or postal orders promptly recorded, and each item delivered should be date stamped and initialled. All items should now be sorted under their appropriate headings. Inter-library loans, periodicals, lending enquiries and administrative post should all be separated and distributed to the departments concerned. Finally, the empty envelopes should be checked to see that nothing has been missed, before clearing away.

Outgoing post should be separated into external and internal. Internal post will be distributed according to local arrangements, and external post through the normal Post Office services. Letters and parcels should be separated, and then each stamped with the correct postage values. Large libraries may use franking machines for this, if the volume of post is sufficient. Before posting, details of the outgoing mail are entered in a postage book, to record the number of stamps used and letters sent. Library postal assistants should become familiar with the full range of Post Office services, set out in the *Post Office guide*, which should be readily available. In particular, staff should know the correct charges for parcels, printed papers, recorded delivery and express services.

Telephones
Just as library assistants working at the issue counter help to create a good impression of the library, so does the handling of telephone calls and callers. Many new telephone systems are now being installed with a range of facilities in addition to just making and receiving calls. It is important that all staff understand and are proficient at using these new facilities such as redirecting calls to other extensions, so that calls are not lost. Enquiries should be dealt with promptly, courteously and efficiently at all times. A note pad and pen should be available next to each telephone, so that staff are ready to deal with calls immediately. When answering calls always give the name of your library and of your department clearly and deliberately, and follow this with a greeting. Identify your caller correctly and write down the name, date and time of the call. Listen to what the caller says and make brief notes. Ask for further details, if the information given is not sufficient, and then read back to the caller the message you have written down. If the caller has to be kept waiting, give reassurances from time to time, so that the caller knows that the request is being dealt with, and that he has not been cut off, or simply ignored. Finally, if the query cannot be dealt with immediately, write down the caller's own telephone number, offer to ring him back; and where necessary outline the steps that will be taken in the meantime.

Telex
Telex is a message transmitting service that can be rented through British Telecom. This national and international service operates through a teleprinter machine designed to transmit and receive messages from similar machines connected by telephone cables.

It is operated in the same way as a typewriter, and to send a message to another subscriber a connection is first made by obtaining a line. The call number of the receiving organization is dialled, and the transmission can then proceed. As the message is being typed on one machine, it is also being reproduced at the receiving end. Printed copies of messages and requests are reproduced at both ends, providing a permanent record of the original request and of the information provided in reply.

Modern telex terminals may have communications ports fitted so that other items of electronic office equipment such as word processors can communicate directly with other telex users without the need to retype messages on the teleprinter. Similarly, incoming messages can be received and distributed internally to the appropriate people for immediate attention.

Electronic Mail
Electronic Mail is a system of communication between computers or terminals linked by telephone lines. Messages are sent via a keyboard to destinations which are identified by numbered codes. The message is thus held in a central computer postbox until the recipient calls up his number to see if there are any messages waiting. Messages can then be read from a visual display unit, down loaded onto disk or printed out onto paper if necessary. Only the person with the identification code number can receive the mail.

Computer messages are transmitted by telephone via a modem which converts the information into digital signals. The central computer holding the information until it is required can supply additional facilities such as simultaneous transmissions to several destinations, and delayed timing to take advantage of off-peak charges. *Telecom Gold* is a large, national system run by British Telecom offering many of these message handling facilities which may be quite expensive to use. Many school and college libraries will have access to *The Times Network Systems* (TTNS) at reduced rates for educational use.

Subscribers are offered a combination of the best features of the telephone and the typewriter; speed plus the authority of the printed word. Users are able to send and receive virtually any form of printed message, and facsimile (FAX) machines are now available which can send and receive exact copies of material such as drawings, diagrams, graphs and handwritten notes.

Telephone callers may be misunderstood, but Electronic Mail gives a written message which can be referred to whenever necessary. Moreover, the receiving end does not need to be manned constantly, for messages can be stored over a weekend or during evenings until required.

Electronic Mail can be used by libraries to supply information in answer to requests from other users. It can be used to communicate with other libraries for interlending and other purposes. It is a quick and accurate method of corresponding with any other organization that also subscribes.

Letters

Official letters are usually written or typed on notepaper already printed with the library's address. It is necessary to add the date under this address, and also to show at the top left hand side of the notepaper the name and address of the person to whom the letter is being sent. Most letters will indicate the initials of the writer's name and the typist's initials if different from the sender's. These initials serve as a reference code for your correspondent's use, and help to trace the origin of the letter within large libraries.

Letters usually begin with 'Dear Sir' or 'Dear Madam' or the person's name or title. Level with this salutation and arranged centrally on the page, it is useful to include an underlined heading informing your correspondent of the subject of your letter.

The body of the letter will consist of short well arranged paragraphs, each of which will deal with one topic only. If the impersonal 'Sir' or 'Madam' has been used, then the letter should end 'Yours faithfully,'. If someone's name has been used at the opening of the letter, then the ending should be 'Yours sincerely,'. Under the signature, the name of the person signing the letter should be written or typed, along with the official position of that person.

When referring to a letter, note the date and reference of the letter that has been received, so that the reply can be immediately matched with the original letter, e.g. 'Thank you for your letter, dated November 23rd, (ref HCA/AE)...' The original letter should be systematically scanned and notes made of items to be included in the reply. Notemaking is made easier by ascertaining what the enquirer needs to know, what else is needed to answer this and what details must be checked before a reply can be prepared. When letters are making requests, notes should be made of each item associated with the subject in hand, including what questions need to be asked and what additional information should be supplied to enable the correspondent to answer your questions adequately. Notes should be reviewed and each item numbered as it will appear in the letter, so as to ensure an organized, logical sequence of ideas.

Short, simple sentences help the contents of the letter to be understood quickly and easily. Also, they are constructed more easily than longer, complex sentences and are more likely to be grammatically correct. A good dictionary should always be at hand, and used whenever the slightest doubt about the spelling of words exists. Jargon should be avoided at all times, and long words should not be used when shorter ones will convey the meaning equally well. Punctuation should be treated as an aid to understanding, and used appropriately.

On completion, the letter should be re-read, and checked to ensure that handwriting is legible throughout, and that the typing is an accurate version of the original. The letter needs checking for the correct address, that enquiries have been properly answered, and that relevant information has been supplied. Grammar, spelling and signature should also be checked, and any enclosures noted. These short simple steps should be followed consistently at all times, to ensure well written and efficient correspondence.

Office machinery
In modern offices a range of clerical and administrative work is increasingly aided by the use of office machinery of different kinds. Where the work is routine or repetitive, office machines can save considerable time and effort on the part of office workers. Often the accuracy and quality of work produced is improved, and the appearance of written and numerical work is enhanced.

Almost every library office will contain a *typewriter* for general as well as specifically library clerical work. There are many makes and sizes of typewriter depending on the kind of work required. *Silent typewriters* can be purchased for rooms where too much noise is a disadvantage, such as public reading rooms, or busy offices where telephones are frequently in use. Most modern offices use *electric typewriters* which are less tiring for their operators, and give an evenness of touch which improves the quality of carbon copies or duplicated stencils. *Electric variable typewriters* which offer interchangeable sizes and styles of type can also be obtained. Line and word spaces can be adjusted so that the finished work looks very similar to letterpress printing. These machines are used for high quality work such as bibliographies, booklists and publicity work. Some modern typewriters have miniature display screens so that users can see what they have typed before printing. Some also have small electronic memories for storing information that is frequently used, such as names and addresses of suppliers, which can then be included without keyboarding them on every occasion they are required.

Word processors allow numbers, letters or words to be retained in a computer style memory so that they can be altered, rearranged or edited after they have been typed. Characters are typed on a keyboard and projected on to a screen called a visual display unit, so that the operator can correct or rearrange what is shown before the final version is printed. Word processors are used mainly for repetitive work with uniform contents which can be made to appear individual or distinctive by the addition of names and addresses or other personal details, or for preliminary versions of letters, minutes and reports which can be easily amended or revised.

Software is now available that can check spelling and punctuation for accuracy, and then correct any typing mistakes! Many word processing machines are specially designed for this purpose, but word processing programs can be obtained for use with most microcomputers with sufficient electronic memory capacity to be viable.

Desk Top Publishing (DTP) software is available for use with high quality laser printers to give good quality design and print facilities for library publications or promotional material.

Electronic office
In a modern, automated office, staff may work at computer terminals linked together and to a central computer providing information for use by everyone. For instance, the record that is

created when a book is ordered can be stored for use again when that book is catalogued, and again when it is issued, rather than separate records being created for each purpose. Each computer terminal can use software to deal with the same information in different ways. Some libraries now have public access systems which allow readers to access computer catalogues and issue systems online to search for material, or make issue enquiries.

Computers can use and rearrange information very quickly, and they bring an accuracy and consistency that takes much of the drudgery out of routine operations such as filing in alphabetical order, writing overdues and addressing envelopes for mailing lists. Unfortunately computers still cannot clear tables and shelve books!

Duplicating

Often, multiple copies of either hand- or typewritten documents are required in libraries. Simple carbon copies can easily be made when routine typing or clerical work is done. If, however, several copies are needed then other methods can be used according to the amount and quality required. *Spirit duplicators* are cheap and easy to use. A master is prepared by writing or typing on to paper which has a carbon backing. The master is fixed to the drum of a small duplicating machine, which is rotated by hand, leaving carbon copies on spirit dampened copy paper. This method is convenient and quick for short runs, and is used extensively in schools and colleges for question papers, diagrams and short notes. Colours can be added by using different carbons. Alterations are difficult to make, and the general appearance and quality is only fair, although it is adequate for the work described. *Stencil duplicating* is very common in libraries and is used extensively for bibliographies, booklists, overdue and reserve notices, minutes, reports and newsletters. A master copy is produced by typing, or writing with a stylus, on a wax stencil, which is then fixed to the drum of a duplicating machine and inked. The drum is rotated, and inked copies are produced on specially absorbent duplicating paper. Electronic stencils can be made so that diagrams, pictures and even half-tone photographs can also be reproduced. Electronic stencils are quite expensive and can be used for cover illustrations, or whenever very long runs are needed. Wax stencils are easy to alter, by using correcting

107

fluid, and can produce good quality, lengthy runs quite cheaply.

Office printing is sometimes done by an *offset litho* machine. Thin metal or paper plate masters are prepared, usually by typing with a special greasy ribbon. The master plates are fixed to the printing machine and copies are produced on the principle of the aversion of water to grease. The moistened plate remains clear of ink as it rotates around cylinders, and the greasy typing picks up the special litho ink which is offset on to a rubber roller, and then on to paper. The paper plates are quite cheap, and the process gives high quality work for very long runs of up to 50,000 copies, using metal plates for the longest runs.

Photocopying

Photocopying machines provide exact copies of original material without the preparation of master plates, and with complete accuracy. They are frequently used for copies from books and journals, as well as for diagrams, charts and normal office copying. Most photocopying machines are easy to use, and are quick and cheap for small numbers of copies. Some machines use a photographic process for which special fluids or papers are required, and these can be messy and inconvenient. Other machines require the original document to enter and pass through the machine, and these of course are unsuitable for library copying.

Electrostatic copiers are becoming increasingly popular in offices and libraries. Copies are produced directly on to ordinary paper by an electric charge, and there are no fluids or negatives involved. *Xerography* is one of the commonest electrostatic processes. Copies are quickly produced, but a large volume of work is needed to justify the costs incurred, and often machines are supplied on rental. All photocopying machines need careful usage, and regular cleaning and maintenance. The numbers and types of copies taken should be recorded, and regular checks made on the amount of stationery or supplies needed.

Copyright

The Copyright (Libraries) Regulations were issued by the Board of Trade in 1957 to regulate the supply of photocopies to readers in public and educational libraries in Great Britain. Briefly, as the law stands, only single copies can be supplied for the purposes of research or private study, on payment of a fee 'not less than the cost (including a contribution to the general expenses of the library) attributable to their production'. Readers who require copies should be asked to sign a copyright undertaking (Figure 5) and should be charged the appropriate fee before the copying is done.

Due to the increase in technology and facilities available since 1957, the law of copyright in Britain has stood in need of revision for some time. The Whitford Committee reported in 1977 on ways to amend the law, but legislation did not follow. Another Government Report entitled *Intellectual property and innovation* has now been published and legislation is expected soon to amend the present law of copyright with regard to photocopying, and the role and use of audio and video recording equipment and materials, and also to extend similar legal protection to computer software.

Data protection
The Data Protection Act, 1984 is concerned with personal information stored and processed by computers. Individual persons are given certain rights by the Act, and computer users must observe obligations which are described as Data Protection Principles. The Principles stipulate that personal data:

a) shall be obtained and processed fairly and lawfully;
b) shall only be stored for specified and lawful purposes, and shall not be used for any other purposes;
c) shall be adequate, relevant and not excessive for the purpose it is held;
d) shall be accurate and kept up-to-date;
e) shall not be kept longer than necessary.
and f) Individuals are entitled to access any personal information about them, and to have this data corrected or erased.
g) Security measures must be taken to prevent unauthorized access to such information.

All computerized personal information and its uses must be registered with the Data Protection Registry so that persons may gain access to information about themselves which is held in computer systems. It is a criminal offence to misuse personal data

109

STOCKPORT COLLEGE OF TECHNOLOGY

To: THE COLLEGE LIBRARIAN

1. I..

    of.. Dept

    hereby request you to make and supply to me the following:
    (N.B. Please quote inclusive page reference)

    ....copies of......................

    ....

    ....

    ....

    ....

    ....

    ....

    which I require for the purpose of research or private study.

2. I have not previously been supplied with a copy by any
    Librarian.

3. I undertake that if a copy is supplied to me in compliance
    with the request made above, I will not use it except for the
    purpose of research or private study.

    SIGNATURE ....

    DATE......................................

Figure 5: Specimen photocopy application form

and individuals may be entitled to compensation if damage is caused by inaccurate information or unauthorized disclosure of such information.

Data security requirements for libraries should include the physical security and access to computer equipment, software security including the use of passwords and restrictions on access to sensitive data, and working practices such as the storage and disposal of printout materials. Personal information which staff may obtain in the course of their work is confidential, and disclosure of such information to unauthorized persons is a very serious matter.

Microreaders
Microreaders are machines to enable the different kinds of microforms to be magnified for reading. There should be machines available for reading every kind of microform held by the library. In a large library this will include 35mm and 16mm roll film, microfiche and microcard. Microreading equipment is not complicated, and library staff should be familiar with its use, and particularly with the interchanging of bulbs, lenses and other carriage components needed for reading the different formats. Many machines are now modified to accept roll film in cassette form, which simplifies usage, and eliminates threading. Some sophisticated machines have motorized winding and instant photocopying facilities. Computer catalogues in large libraries are often produced on microfiche or on microfilm in cassettes, for use by staff and public on suitable microreaders.

Audio-visual equipment
In educational libraries especially there may be collections of audio-visual material for use by readers. All the necessary audio-visual equipment should be available for use with each type of material held (e.g. slide, film and filmstrip projectors, radio and television sets, audio and video recorders, with the appropriate monitors and playing equipment). Complicated equipment for using interactive video discs which allow random access to recorded information, or online computer databases with elaborate protocols, or even microcomputers on open access may present problems for members of the public, and therefore all library staff should be properly trained to operate all the

equipment available and to anticipate simple software problems. They should also be able to perform simple, routine maintenance such as replacing ribbons, changing bulbs, and setting up paper printers, rewinding and repairing tapes, and adjusting or replacing record styli, in order to provide a fully comprehensive range of services and assistance to readers at all times.

Assignments
1 Describe briefly a method dealing with incoming and outoing mail in a library. State the type of library. (CGLI 1981)
2 Explain the correct way to deal with a telephone enquiry. (CGLI 1979)
3 Describe *each* of the pieces of office equipment detailed below, explaining how each benefits the organization and routines of a library:
   a a photocopying machine
   b a microfiche reader
   c a tape typewriter
   d a telex machine.
   (CGLI 1980)
4 List some of the advantages of using telex as a means of communication in libraries. Give examples from your own experience where relevant. (CGLI 1986)
5 Why is it important that office practices be efficiently performed in a library system? Illustrate by quoting specific examples. (CGLI 1971)

FURTHER READING

ANTHONY, L.J. *ed.*   *Handbook of special librarianship and information work*, 5th ed, ASLIB, 1983.

ASHWORTH, W.   *Special librarianship*, Bingley, 1979.

BROWN, R.   *Public library administration*, Bingley, 1979.

CHERNIK, B.E.   *Procedures for library media technical assistants*, ALA, 1983.

CORBETT, E.V.   *Fundamentals of library organization and administration*, LA, 1978.

FOTHERGILL, R. and BUTCHART, I.   *Non-book materials in libraries*, 2nd ed. Bingley, 1984.

HARRISON, C. and BEENHAM, R.   *The basics of librarianship*, 2nd ed. Bingley, 1985.

HARRISON, K.C.   *First steps in librarianship*, 5th rev.ed. Deutsch, 1980.

HERRING, J.E.   *School librarianship*, 1st ed. Bingley, 1982. (2nd ed., 1988)

HIGGENS, G. *ed.*   *Printed reference material*, 2nd ed. LA, 1984.

HUNTER, E.J. and BAKEWELL, K.   *Cataloguing*, 2nd ed. Bingley, 1982.

KELLY, T.   *History of public libraries in Great Britain, 1845-1975*, 2nd ed. LA, 1977.

LIBRARY ASSOCIATION   *Professional and non-professional duties in libraries*, 2nd ed. 1974.

McELROY, A.R. *ed.*   *College librarianship*, LA, 1984.

PRYTHERCH, R.   *The basics of readers' advisory work*, Bingley, 1987.

RAY, S.G.	*Children's librarianship*, Bingley, 1979.
RAY, S.G.	*Library services to schools*, 3rd ed. LA, 1982.
ROWLEY, J.	*Computers for libraries*, 2nd ed. Bingley, 1985.
	School libraries: the foundations of the curriculum, HMSO, 1984.
STIRLING, J.F. *ed.*	*University librarianship*, LA, 1981.

AUTHOR NOTES

Both authors began their careers as library assistants, and both have taught library assistants for many years.

Phyllis Oldfield was formerly a lecturer in Library Studies at Stockport College of Technology. She is an Open University graduate, a Chartered Librarian and a qualified teacher. She has taught in schools for many years, and school libraries are a particular interest. She has been secretary of the Greater Manchester branch of the School Library Association for many years and she has also served on the Association's national committee. Now retired, she is actively involved in in-service training for school librarians in the north west of England.

John Chirgwin is College Librarian and a principal lecturer at Stockport College of Technology. He is a graduate, a Chartered Librarian and a qualified teacher. He has been employed in further education for over 20 years, both in England and Scotland.

Index